M000027749

LYME RAGE

A Mother's Struggle to Save Her Daughter
From Lyme Disease

LYME RAGE

A Mother's Struggle to Save Her Daughter
From Lyme Disease

Mindy Haber

Epigraph Publishing Service
Rhinebeck, NY

Lyme Rage: A Mother's Struggle to Save Her Daughter From Lyme Disease
Copyright © 2014 Mindy Haber
All rights reserved. No part of this book may be used or reproduced in any manner without written permission from the author except in critical articles and reviews.

Contact the publisher for information.

Book and cover design by Chris Hallman
Cover Photography: Elizabeth Fox

ISBN: 978-1-936940-91-2
Ebook: 978-1-936940-92-9

Printed in the United States of America
Library of Congress Control Number: 2014944958

AUTHOR'S NOTE: The following is the story of my experiences as a parent trying to navigate through the onset, advancement, symptoms, diagnosis and treatment of my daughter's lyme disease. I am not a doctor and this book is not meant to suggest any diagnosis or endorse any treatment for lyme or related tick borne illnesses. While I believe that an earlier diagnosis of my daughter's symptoms should have been made, I do not seek to malign any health care professionals who treated her. —Mindy Haber

A 5% contribution from the profits of the sale of this book will go to helping victims of Lyme disease.

Epigraph Books
22 East Market Street, Suite 304
Rhinebeck, NY 12572
www.epigraphps.com

This book is dedicated to my three daughters,
Casey, Molly, Sophie, and to
all the victims of Lyme disease,
Never, never, never give up.

Acknowledgements

I want to thank my family for putting up with me during this labor intensive process of putting this story together on paper. It was a great sacrifice for them. Thanks to my daughter Casey for being the first person to read the whole story and give me her unyielding support. Peter, thanks for reading the story and accepting my view of you in this journey, without judgment. Thanks Molly for your forgiveness. For you Sophie, I thank you because you inspired me to be the best person I could ever be in this life and for making me realize what is truly important in life-living it to the fullest. To my mother, Rochelle, I thank you for making me a persevering person who never gives up.

Thank you Wendy Wynberg LCSW, for reading the manuscript and giving me your support and help with understanding what I was trying to convey to make it better. To Maria LoCastro LCSW, thank you for being my friend, reading the story and confirming that it was indeed my authentic voice.

To all my co-workers, you know who you are, thank you for listening daily about my daughter's predicament and giving your full support. To all of you for asking me day after day, "How is Sophie doing?" providing me your kindness and compassion over the years of Sophie's illness. I am forever in your debt.

Thanks to all the healthcare professionals that participated in giving Sophie and our family hope.

Thanks to Epigraph Publishing, particularly Anastasia McGhee for gently leading me into the journey of getting this story published.

Table of Contents

Much Madness is Divinest Sense

Much Madness is divinest sense
To a discerning Eye;
Much Sense - the starkest Madness.

'Tis the Majority
In this, as all, prevails.

Assent, and you are sane;
Demur, —you're straightaway dangerous,
And handled with a Chain.

—Emily Dickinson

The resolution to avoid an evil is seldom framed till the evil is so far advanced as to make avoidance impossible.

—Thomas Hardy

Introduction

I never thought my life would travel into tragedy. However, there are events that occur unexpectedly. There was an illness that took over my life, and it changed me. The world turned like a merry-go-round, day after day, until the illness happened. The life that was familiar to me had hit a dead end. I was thrown off course into a deep, dark pit.

Lyme disease had captured my daughter. I failed to realize that the random symptoms she was experiencing had anything to do with Lyme disease. Every time I took my daughter to the emergency room at the local hospital, each symptom was treated as a separate problem, and I didn't have enough information about Lyme disease to realize that these symptoms were all connected.

I could not have known, rushing to the hospital when Sophie was coughing uncontrollably, gasping for breath, that coughing was just one affliction on a long list of random symptoms that are related to Lyme disease. Nor could I have known that Lyme disease was causing the hammer-banging headache she once had for several days, and required a visit to the emergency room without receiving a clear explanation as to the cause from the doctors.

I had no idea what to do the time Sophie had a gut-wrenching, screeching outburst while lying on the gurney in the emergency room, screaming, "HELP

ME, MOMMY, HELP ME! GET IT OUT OF ME! PLEASE, MOMMY, GET IT OUT OF ME!" Those words burst forth with rage from her lips. There was terror in her dark, brown eyes, which were piercing me like daggers, begging me to do something, anything to get this awful thing out of her. She looked like a psychotic, feral child. Little did I know, she was being invaded by bacteria, crossing the blood-brain barrier to wreck her mind. I had no idea that the neurological effects of Lyme disease were what were turning my daughter away from being a happy, carefree child.

Sophie became sick with Lyme disease when she was nine years old. I did not know the devastating results of the disease. The symptoms and potential problems associated with Lyme disease had never been discussed when I'd taken my daughter to the pediatrician for routine physicals, so when she got sick, I was lost. Every doctor we encountered couldn't give a clear diagnosis of the random variation of symptoms my daughter was experiencing. It was horrifying.

I had been walking along the path of life and had suddenly fallen into a trap: my daughter's illness. Was I prepared to go the distance, do whatever it took to get her well? Would I be able to beat the odds when they were against me? Could I have known what would happen next? My daughter had been sucked into a black hole, and I was reaching around in the dark, trying in desperation to pull her out.

I felt lost and had no guide telling me which way to go. There were no words that could explain the awful feeling of doom that I felt. I was speechless and totally alone. Nothing else mattered but this little person—my child, my daughter.

As my family and I waited for answers, my life was falling apart, hanging by a thread. Questions kept flooding me, but not one doctor seemed to know what was happening. I wanted to scream out, "Why don't you know, why can't you help my child, why, why, why?" The only response I got was a voice in my head telling me that my daughter was getting sicker and would wither away into nothingness. My mind was on a continuous IV drip of dreadful thoughts.

The days no longer had a beginning or an end, each one falling into the next. Sleep was troublesome at best, food had no taste, and all I could do was limp along, trying to act normal, trying to be like everyone else, but it wasn't working. I didn't have the energy to hate or blame or point the finger at the individuals who could not help my child.

There were tests, but they did not yield answers. I felt like I was running out of luck. I wanted so desperately to believe that I had this whole thing wrong. Why was it that the doctors did not know what to do?

What does the evidence say about Lyme disease and other tick-borne illnesses, and where could we find it? Does the American Medical Association even know the various symptoms that emerge from tick bites? Does the Center for Disease Control know what is really happening to people getting sick from ticks? And who had the responsibility to provide the information about the bacteria transmitted by ticks and the multitude of medical issues people are suffering? Is it all just experimental?

Doctors often behave in ways that make us believe they have answers. That's the problem with Lyme disease. So many doctors don't really know what to do to about it. Why was it that many of the doctors in an identified endemic area would not even consider the possibility of Lyme disease?

I hold out a small piece of hope for doctors out there willing to challenge the status quo of medicine. They embark upon uncharted territory to save lives.

To Live without hope is to cease to live.

—Fyodor Dostoevsky

Once upon a time there was a nine-year-old girl named Sophie. Her life was like a fairytale. She was a happy-go-lucky, fun-loving, free-spirited child.

Sophie had pin-straight, light brown hair that could fly in the wind and land exactly where it had been before, straight and in its place. She had deep, dark brown eyes, perfectly structured eyebrows, and a smile so big that it could reach around the world. She loved to laugh and play and never had a worry. Sophie was always happy. Her teachers described her as a kind person, always willing to help other students. Sophie's parents identified her as a compassionate and creative child. She was considerate of others, friendly, yet had a mind of her own. She spread joy wherever she went, like generous portions of peanut butter and jelly on bread.

Sophie loved to discover the world. She was curious about how stuff worked, and was always asking questions about everything—about the stars, the sky, her endless encounters with life's happenings and the people she met. Sophie bombarded her parents with her ideas. But most of all, she loved to help people.

Sophie's family consisted of her mother, Mindy, her father, Peter, her two older sisters, Casey and Molly, and two family dogs, Cody and Daisy. Molly lived at home, but was often busy at school or was out of the house socializing. Casey was away at college in Upstate New York, and was soon to be graduating and leaving for graduate school in California. So, like an only child, Sophie enjoyed the devotion of her parents as they provided her with all the attention and care she needed. She did not want for anything.

Sophie's parents decided to move to a more secluded area of the Hudson Valley. They had lived in the area for the past ten years and had been planning to move for a while. Together, they had found a place where they could build their new home, enveloped by lush greenery as far as the eye could see. They hoped the seclusion of the wooded area would provide their daughter with the promise of cultivating a sense of her free-spirited self. Sophie would be able to wander in the forest—it would be her new play land. Abundant trees and bushes filled the pathways through the green-covered mountains and valleys. Sophie would be able to venture into the world of the woods. In this place, her curiosity could unfold.

When Sophie was told the news of the move, she was delighted. She was so excited when her parents showed her the pictures of their new home and she discovered that she would have so much free space to create adventures.

When they finally arrived in their new place, Sophie could not help herself, she was compelled to venture out into the picturesque garden of green. The first thing Sophie noticed were the sounds of the birds, each singing a soliloquy of their own. Together the birds seemed to create an orchestra. She also noticed creatures milling along the stone driveway. Each creature appeared to be on its own mission, crawling along with microscopic steps. It seemed to take an eternity for each little creature to move from one piece of gravel to another. In this new place, Sophie discovered that there was a rhythm in nature that was critically important to each creature—one by one, they slowly moved along, seeking to conquer the ground beneath them. Sophie could watch nature's little creatures, those tiny specs of living things, for hours in this new wonderland.

Entranced by this new place, Sophie was fascinated by all the animal life that surrounded her. She loved to play outside, following the dirt pathways through the thick, wiry branches leading into the woods. Peter would often lure her into the woods to find his lost golf balls. Like two adventurers, they would walk to the end of the path behind their home, bend their heads, and disappear into the massive greenery of the woods. After what seemed like hours, the two of them would suddenly emerge from the thick, sprawling vegetation and walk back to the house with a bucket half-filled with golf balls. They would be talking and laughing together, and after resting, they would get ready to do it all over again. It was joyous to watch them on their adventure.

Sometimes they would return with a friend of Sophie's who lived somewhere on the other side of the woods. Happiness grew everywhere. Those were the days of laughing, and singing, walking through the woods and flower picking. Just sitting outside and watching the sun edging across the trees as it went down was so comforting. The plush, green forestry was a magnificent garden of nature's beauty, surrounding Sophie at all times and bringing great joy to her family.

But little did the family know, there was a monstrous creature of microscopic proportions watching them from the deep, dark green forest. It was a tiny arachnid that was able to thrive in these woods. The story told was that these little creatures were catching rides on deer and white-footed mice to get to humans. It is human blood that this little creature thirsted for and sought to conquer. All a human had to do to be invaded by this tiny, miserable creature was to go into the woods. The family had not realized that the place they had moved to was not just another town in the country—it was an area where these terrible creatures lived and thrived en masse. These little passengers, ticks, brought sickness to people. Many were aware of the illness that could occur if they were bitten by infected ticks, but no one knew how bad the sickness could get, or recognize the types of symptoms that could surface.

The family didn't know and couldn't have anticipated that having journeyed into this unforgiving land their lives would be changed forever. They had left Fairyland and had unknowingly entered into a foreign habitat of great misfortune, a place known as Tickland.

The end.

Fear is the mother of foresight.

—Thomas Hardy

I am Sophie's mother and it is my mission to tell you about the journey I took to save my daughter from Lyme disease—the illness that took my little girl away from being the happy person she was. It all started with two tick bites that the medical world nonchalantly shrugged off as nothing important.

I have always believed that doctors are people you can trust. They have always have been the ultimate authority when I, or someone I love, had been sick. So I trusted Sophie's doctors. I was at their mercy, and emphatically believed that they held the answers I needed to get my child well. It was shocking to find out that the doctors did not have the answers and painful to realize that many doctors knew very little about Lyme disease and its devastation. In fact, many doctors minimized Sophie's symptoms and were unable to put the pieces together to create an accurate picture of her illness.

Watching Lyme disease ravage my daughter's body and mind was almost impossible to endure and was one of the most painful periods of my life. Wrapped in my daughter's sickness, I was left scrounging around, trying to scrape my way out and find a path to wellness.

My mind clouds when I try to remember how it all began. When I start to think about it my eyes fill up with tears. How did it all start? When did my daughter Sophie begin to get sick?

In 2009, over the Christmas holiday break, we took a family trip to Disney World. Sophie enjoyed the trip very much, although she complained often of headaches. When this happened I would give her some Motrin or Tylenol. I hardly even noticed the pattern of headaches that was insidiously sneaking up on her. It never dawned on me to question how frequent these headaches were becoming. I thought that giving her the over-the-counter remedy would solve the problem. I didn't see that there was some change occurring. How could I know anything was really different? Yet looking back, I realize that Sophie had complained of a headache almost every night we were at Disney World. At the time, I told myself it was probably because of the long days of going on rides and walking through parks. So I handed out the remedies and my daughter took them without question. Often she would fall asleep afterwards and sleep peacefully through the night.

Was there any real, substantial clue to tell me that my daughter was getting sick? How could I have possibly known that this was the beginning of an illness that was more dangerous than anything she or I had ever experienced? How could I have realized that this was something I needed to be concerned about from the start?

After returning from Disney World, Sophie went back to school. Late in January 2010, she developed a really bad cough. When I think back, she also seemed to be looking pale. . .

How could I have been so blind? Why didn't I recognize that the changes occurring were significant? Could I have caught the disease sooner? Sophie never had a cough like this one. It was harsh, loud, and barking—the kind of a cough that could come from inhaling a toxic substance. It was so deep it sounded as if her ribs could crack at any moment. Soon it made me feel frightened. It was as if I could visualize Sophie's bronchial pathways being clogged with smoke from a fire. The cough would not let go of her. I decided to take her to the pediatrician, which is what I would normally do under these circumstances. So off we went to the doctor.

At the pediatric practice where my daughter was treated, we did not always see the same doctor. Whenever we went to the doctor's office, we would wait until we were called into the exam room where we would wait some more until the doctor arrived. While waiting, we would play games, dance, tell jokes and stories, make funny faces and laugh. But for this visit, we did not do that because all Sophie could do was cough, cough, and cough some more. I held her cheek and tried to comfort her as we waited. She just kept coughing, and between coughs, she told me that her chest hurt, her throat hurt, her body hurt.

Finally, the doctor arrived in the exam room. She looked at Sophie, then at me, and began asking questions, trying to assess the problem. Usually the visit took about fifteen minutes, but this one went much longer than usual. I had never met this doctor before. The doctor examined Sophie and then asked whether my daughter had ever had asthma, to which I responded, "No, my daughter has never been diagnosed with asthma." The pediatrician looked at me perplexed, as if I was not telling her the truth. "Come on," I thought to myself, "why are you questioning me?" I was beginning to wonder whether this doctor had any skills at all. "You don't know the answer," I thought to myself, "so you look suspiciously at me."

I was dumbfounded over the confusing, wordless body language taking place between the doctor and me—after which the doctor told me, in a confident tone, that she was prescribing an albuterol inhaler. I was too tired to argue, so I acquiesced. Whether the inhaler would help my little girl feel relief, I did not know. I had no choice but to proceed to the pharmacy to get the medication.

I made the copayment at the front desk, and together we strolled down the stairs and out into the brisk evening air. I told Sophie that we needed to fill the prescription before we could go home. She was exhausted and continued to cough. Sophie shrugged her shoulders, which is what she usually does when she isn't feeling well. The shrug means that she is okay with whatever I need to do, I have come to learn. So off we went, down the road to the pharmacy.

At the pharmacy, Sophie was still coughing badly and did not want to go inside, so I went through the drive-thru to get the prescription filled. As we waited together in the car, her cough went on, as nagging as an itchy mosquito bite, barely letting her catch her breath. I attempted to talk to her, but talking just caused more coughing, so I stayed quiet and watched her coughing next to me. I felt anxious, and hoped that the inhaler would give her some relief so she could go to sleep when we got home.

Finally, we went back to the drive-thru window to pick up the medication. Hoping that it would be the magic key to end the coughing, I told Sophie it would be okay and zoomed off toward home. It was a relief to get there, and we rushed inside the house. I opened the package with the inhaler, tore it out of its package, and showed her how to use the inhaler. Then Sophie took the inhaler in her hands, put the open part into her mouth, and got ready to breathe in as she pressed her fingers down on the pump. She took two puffs and handed the inhaler to me. I told her to get into her pajamas for bed. Again she offered that solemn shrug, so tired and limp but compliant. I watched her walk down the hallway to her room and then I went off to get myself in order.

About thirty minutes later, I heard a frantic voice telling me that she couldn't stop coughing. Between each word there was a cough. A heart-pounding adrenaline rush stilled me. Sophie could not get hold of her breath. She was barely able to vocalize the difficulty she was having breathing. I looked at her, knowing that I had to make a decision quickly as to what to do next. Then I told her, in a firm but frantic tone, to put on her jacket because we were going to the hospital. She was hesitant and frightened, but nevertheless, she got her jacket. I rushed to get my coat on, feeling adrenaline pump through my body as we moved out the door and into the car once again. Sophie got into the back seat, gasping for air. She was coughing harder than ever now—the kind of gut-wrenching, dry-heaving, body-clenching hold that tenses every muscle in your body until you are as stiff as a piece of wood. But she wasn't only coughing. In the rearview mirror I could see that she was also crying in spurts.

All the way to the hospital, Sophie continued coughing, telling me with each breath possible that she could not breathe. I raced down the road, feeling my heart pounding and my own breaths getting shorter. As my daughter's body twitched from bronchial spasms and her airways closed up, I realized that I was hyperventilating. I felt frantic, paralyzed, yet I continued to drive. I was on autopilot and in a kind of trance—moving, but numb. I felt terribly helpless.

I decided to call the pediatric group to say I needed help. The person who answered told me a nurse would call me back. "This is an emergency!" I said. The person told me to hold on and I waited, on the verge of exploding with anxiety as Sophie continued to cough. Finally the person returned and told me again that a nurse would call me back. I wanted to scream, but no sound materialized. I shut off my cell phone, then realized that if someone called back I would be unreachable, so I turned it back on.

A few minutes passed. Beads of sweat ran down my forehead. I continued to exceed the speed limit. Somehow, miraculously, there were no cops around to stop me. Finally the nurse called back. I told her quickly what was happening to Sophie. The nurse told me to keep her talking until we got to the hospital. "As long as she is talking, she will be okay," the nurse said. "If your daughter starts turning blue, then you need to worry about whether she is breathing."

"Okay," I replied, feeling my own breathing accelerate even more.

I watched Sophie in the rearview mirror. Turning blue is the sign of not getting enough oxygen. This information terrified me. I felt out of my league, in total, undeniable panic. But I told myself I had to be strong for Sophie and kept driving. Finally, we reached the hospital. I found the closest parking spot, jumped out of the car, and helped Sophie get out. Together we walked inside.

As we entered the Emergency Room, a nurse came out of her cubicle and immediately yelled out, "Respiratory distress!" She was talking about Sophie, I realized with some small particle of relief. The nurse brought us into the cubicle and took Sophie's vital signs, which were within normal limits, thank God. But Sophie was still coughing hard, and she complained to the nurse that it was hurting her throat, neck, and chest. "I'm moving you into a room," the nurse said, and took us to a room with two beds. Sophie sat down on one of the beds. I told her to lie down and make herself comfortable, and then explained to her that we would be there for a while so she needed to try and relax. As we waited for someone to arrive to tell us what would happen next, I sat next to Sophie and held her hand. Within a few minutes, another nurse came in to ask for information about what had been happening this evening. I began to tell the story, and the nurse wrote down the information with a deadpan expression on her face. Somehow I recounted everything that had happened that night prior to and after going to the pediatrician while Sophie lay on the bed, staring at us, still coughing. I watched her as I told the nurse that since the over-the-counter medication had not given her any relief, the pediatrician had recommended an albuterol inhaler, but that hadn't worked either.

The whole time I was talking to the nurse, Sophie kept looking at me for answers, and I kept holding her hand, looking back at her helplessly, because I had no answers. The nurse told me the doctor would be in shortly and left. I kept talking to Sophie, telling her not to worry, that the doctor would help her, that the hospital staff would take care of her, that she would be okay. I spoke calmly, confidently, but I did not really know whether anything I was saying was even true. But somehow I believed it to be true, to be fact. Finally the doctor arrived, asking the same questions all over again. I quickly repeated the story of what had happened that evening to the doctor while he examined Sophie. He decided to give her a nebulizer treatment, and a respiratory therapist came to hook up the tubes and facemask. Medication was put into the contraption, and Sophie was told how to breathe.

I sat there watching Sophie trying to breathe, hoping she would get some relief. But after the treatment, after we had waited a while and there was still no relief, another treatment was ordered. After the second treatment, she was still coughing uncontrollably. Finally, the doctor instructed the nurse to give her prednisone. Again, the nurse put the medication into the contraption connected to Sophie's facemask and she breathed it in. The doctor said she would continue to be treated until the coughing had subsided, which was a relief. After this final treatment, the cough abated. Sophie looked exhausted and told me that she wanted to go home. I told her we had to wait for the doctor to tell us that we could go home and explained that the doctor wanted us to stay a while longer to ensure that the cough would not return.

We waited for about an hour before the doctor came to release Sophie. Finally, her cough had been subdued. Drained and depleted, we moved in slow motion together out into the night, back into the car, and back home, where we were both able to sleep.

And yet to every bad, there is
a worse.

—Thomas Hardy

The Mystery Illness

A few weeks after the coughing episode, Sophie got headaches a few days in a row. As I usually do, I gave her the children's dose of Tylenol and each headache eventually disappeared. However, the headaches kept coming back until they got so bad that Sophie started crying.

"Mom, it hurts really, really bad."

"Can you describe the pain?" I asked.

"I don't know how to explain it, it hurts all over."

"I guess we need to go to the emergency room."

She looked relieved. But I felt helpless, as if I were trapped in a nightmare that kept returning night after night.

"Sophie, go get your jacket on."

I watched her as she walked away. Then I got ready to leave. Sophie followed me out of the house to the car. I clicked the remote to unlock the car door. Together we got into the car and sat down in stony silence, like people getting ready to attend a funeral. With Sophie buckled in next to me, I turned on the engine, checked the rearview mirror, and put on my seatbelt. Then I slowly backed out of the driveway, only to start speeding to the emergency room of the local hospital, once again.

In the emergency room waiting area we sat slumped in our seats, looking down at the floor and around at the empty, forlorn faces of the other people waiting to be seen. I peeked up at Sophie and saw that her expression was filled with pain. After a few minutes, the nurse came out of her cubicle and asked to see us. I told the nurse that Sophie had been having headaches, and that this one was a really bad one. I told her I had given her Tylenol but it did not help relieve the pain, that in fact, the pain had become worse. Sophie began to moan, "It hurts, Mommy, it hurts." I grabbed her hand tighter and leaned toward her, moving closer to her face in a feeble attempt to understand what she was suffering. "I know, I know," I said. But I did not have a clue as to what was happening. The nurse continued with her inquisition, taking Sophie's blood pressure, temperature, and pulse rate, and said nothing seemed out of the ordinary. The nurse told us to take a seat in the waiting room and said Sophie would be seen soon. After a few more minutes, the nurse scurried us into a room within the emergency area. Sophie walked into the room and sat down on one of the beds with a thump, then she lay down. She was wearing an expression on her face that said, "Help!" I grabbed her hand and she gave mine a tight squeeze, which I knew meant that the pain was becoming unbearable. I felt a stabbing pain in my stomach as I watched her lying there with a blank stare. What could I do to help her?

The nurse came back to ask for more information and I talked to her, my head bobbing back and forth from her to my daughter. Sophie was moaning louder and louder, as if she were calling out like a wolf at the full moon. "Where does it hurt the most?" the nurse asked. "My whole head hurts," Sophie said. The nurse said she needed to put an IV into Sophie's hand so that if the doctor wanted to give her medication, she could get it right away. Sophie looked at the nurse and then at me. "Okay," I told the nurse while still looking at Sophie. "Okay, okay," Sophie told the nurse. "You can do it."

The nurse explained that Sophie would feel a pinch and then it would be over. "Ouch!" Sophie said as the IV went into her hand. There was fear in her eyes, but she calmed some when I told her to look at me, not the IV needle. But as the nurse and I tried to reassure her, Sophie told me that the pain hurt so badly she couldn't think about anything else. "It's okay," I said, "Don't worry about it." As we waited for the doctor I held her hand and tried to soothe her pain by pressing the palm of my other hand against her forehead, gently rubbing from side to side the small space above her eyebrows. "It hurts so much," Sophie kept saying over and over.

What was I to do? I couldn't imagine how much pain she was suffering, yet I sat there next to her bed, holding her hand, telling her she would be okay, knowing that I was helpless. As I waited, I felt anxiety rising up inside of me like lava ready to burst from a volcano. But I had to appear calm in the presence of my daughter so for a while I sat complacently and waited. Where was the doctor? I walked to the door, hoping I would see a doctor so I could plead for help, but there was no doctor anywhere to be seen. I stood gaping, as if I had been punched hard in the stomach. Helplessly, I retreated back into the room, sat down, and grabbed my daughter's hand.

As I looked at Sophie, trying to understand what she was feeling at this moment, the doctor arrived. It was a doctor I had never met before, not that I spend much time in the emergency room at the local hospital, but I expected familiarity for some unknown, inexplicable, silly reason. In a low, monotone voice without any inflection, this bald, purplish-looking man, whose face is still lodged in my memory bank, said, "Hello." He reminded me of Uncle Fester from The Addams Family television show. As I stared at him, he looked back at us and said in a matter-of-fact manner, "I think your daughter is having migraines." He presented this statement like it was an epiphany, a moment of grand awakening, as if to say, the final assessment has been made and here it is on a silver platter for you to swallow up.Now what should we do? The doctor went on to explain the procedural options. First, he said she should have a CT scan of her brain, but she should also have a Lyme test. A Lyme test? That wasn't something I had even considered to be a possibility. I traveled with Sophie to another area of the hospital for the CT scan and to the lab for her blood to be taken. I found out later that there are risks associated with CT scans due to exposure to radiation, according to a July 18, 2013 article on the CBS News website, which ran under the headline: "Less Than Half of Parents Aware of CT-Scan Cancer Risk." Yet this procedure was prescribed routinely for my daughter without me being told of the risks.

The results of the CT scan and the Lyme test, the doctor reported, did not provide any findings indicating a problem. But he added, "We have another option for treating the headache. She can be given a pediatric dose of morphine for the pain." It took me a few moments to absorb what he was saying. I thought, "You have got to be kidding me, morphine!?! For a little nine-year-old girl?" I mean, I am not a doctor, but seriously, morphine as the first line of pain management for a nine-year-old child? Was there something wrong with me to question this? Was there something wrong with the doctor for offering this as the first line of treatment for my daughter's headache? "Is there something a little less strong for her to try first?" I asked. "We could try Tylenol with codeine," he said. Were there any other potential alternatives in this situation? I did not have a clue. "Okay, that sounds reasonable," I said.

I felt so naïve, as if I were traveling in uncharted territory. It was as if my thoughts were swishing around and disappearing down a waterhole with a strong current. I was still fighting being taken in by the current, yet it felt too strong. I sat next to Sophie and held her hand while the doctor left the room to tell the nurse what to give my daughter. After the nurse gave Sophie the medication, the doctor returned to tell me to make an appointment with Sophie's pediatrician in the morning. He also recommended that I take my daughter to see a neurologist.

After three hours of being in the hospital, Sophie's pain had hardly subsided. I told her that we were going home. She slowly pulled herself up and turned so that her feet dangled to the floor. I put her jacket on her and we walked out to the car. I wrapped my arm around her, holding her close to my side as we stepped out into the cold, night air. I helped her into the back seat of the car so she could lie down. We traveled quietly home and I got her into the house and into bed.

Somehow I wanted to believe that the Tylenol with codeine had helped her fall asleep rather than total exhaustion. It seemed that waiting the three hours at the hospital had brought her to the brink of collapse, and so she had fallen onto her bed in a stupor as sleep took over her body. I stared at her in her bed. She was peaceful for just that moment. I wanted to cling to that peacefulness, but I was too worried. I thought about what had happened at the hospital and I just didn't know what to believe. I was unable to make sense of her headaches. It was confusing how this illness had accelerated so suddenly, but I was too tired to go through it in my head anymore. So I put my mind on hold to get some sleep. I called Peter to tell him what had happened that evening. Knowing that she was now sleeping, he said, "Whatever it is, it will go away tomorrow." But I wondered, as he spoke to me, which "tomorrow" he was talking about—the next day, next week, or maybe even next year?

When morning arrived Sophie was still complaining of pain, but she said it was not as bad as it had been last night. I needed to determine whether she was able to go to school. I asked her whether she thought that she could get through the school day. Sophie looked at me with indecision written across her face but told me that she would try. So the morning routine took over with Sophie getting dressed and having some oatmeal for breakfast. We talked while she was eating. Then with a face that said, help me, she asked if I could drive her to school. I looked at her. "Why?" She told me that she couldn't deal with the noise on the bus. Her face was as sad as a wilted flower, so I replied, "It's not a problem, I will drive you."

I realized that sound sensitivity was a new addition to the symptom picture that was growing like a sprawling tree, beyond my comprehension. An increasing number of ailments were reaching the surface right before my eyes. I could not imagine what her pain was like, or how her senses were putting her into an agonizing state of despair. All that was left for me to do was to tell Sophie that I loved her. It was important to me that she knew how much I cared about her. When I told her, she stared up at me with a small smile that broke through the sadness momentarily and made me believe that she was going to be okay. I wanted to believe that her illness was just a minor hardship we could conquer together. Hoping that we could climb this mountain of disease together and get to the wellness on the other side. Hope would get us there. It had to. All I had left was hope. Without it, I was empty.

We finally got out of the house and into the car to go to school. As we drove, the silence of our thoughts, like the wind, seemed to howl around us. We were communicating without speaking to one another. I sensed her trepidation as to whether she could make it through another day of school. I stopped the car with a jolt in front of the school. Sophie looked at me as if she had been punched hard in her stomach. I saw pain on her lips as she told me goodbye, barely speaking above a whisper. I watched her walk into the building. Then, looking into the rearview mirror, I saw my face. My eyes were filling up with tears of the pain I had to endure regarding my daughter's predicament.

I drove to work, feeling numb. My mind drifted off into the landscape of this green wilderness where ticks hid on animals that carried them to my doorstep and infected my baby girl. No sooner had I arrived at work, I received a phone call from the school. It was the nurse on the other end of the line, telling me that Sophie was complaining that her head hurt. I knew I had to go get her. Worry began to consume me.

I told my colleagues that I had to leave to get my daughter from school, as she was sick. As I drove the same way back to the school, my mind was racing with thoughts of what to do next.

Feeling lost, I contacted my primary care physician from the school parking lot to ask if he would see Sophie and give me his opinion. The staff member I spoke to said yes, he would.

"We are going to see my doctor because I want to know what he thinks of your headaches," I told Sophie.

"Okay, mom."

I drove as quickly as I could to his office, about fifteen miles from my home. Expeditiously, I parked the car, hopped out with a rush for the answer to my prayers and walked inside his office. A few minutes passed and the doctor came out to hurry us into his office. He's such a caring and compassionate person that I trust, he asked my daughter questions with an attentive, listening ear. The back and forth dialogue with him asking her the questions and her giving the answers was an interlude of caring between two people. Finally, he looked up at me to tell me that he was not a pediatrician so he was unable to prescribe treatment for her, but the symptoms, he retorted, may indicate migraines. In some way, I felt a bit of relief, maybe it was just migraines. If it were migraines, then the neurologist would be able to prescribe treatment. I just wanted to believe that it was migraines. The immediate answer would be simple then, even if it was not the final diagnosis. That was it, I wanted the diagnosis, to know what she had brewing inside her body. Having an answer would be the first step toward treatment options. We left his office only to be confronted with the unnerving pain that was unable to leave my daughter's head. Sophie told me, "Mommy it hurts, my head still hurts." With her lids half closed over her eyes, she looked at me with defeat. She told me that any loud noise was intolerable and made her feel worse. I rushed home to give her some Motrin because she wouldn't take the Tylenol with codeine that they had given her at the hospital. Sophie lay down on her bed, trying to get some relief. I looked at her helpless, motionless body and told her that if she needed me I would be in my room—as if relaxing in my own room would give me solitude and peace of mind. That was a lie I lived with each and every day. There was no peace of mind. My thoughts were always the same: Would I be able to get her better? Was there someone who knew what to do to help my daughter? No matter where I was, I felt as if there was no relief in sight. How could there be, so long as my child was in pain, suffering without the knowledge that there would be an end to this illness?

I walked into my room, plopped down on my side of the bed, and lay there lifeless, looking up at the blank ceiling as if the answers were waiting there for me. I examined each crack, crevice, and dust ball I could find. I felt an awful pang of pain rushing through me as if I'd walked into a rose bush and been pricked all over. I was engrossed in watching time pass me by when I heard a sudden cry: "MA, MA, MA!" I immediately got up like a robot and hurried down the hallway to Sophie's room. She was sitting up in her bed. "Yes?" I said. "What can I do for you?" I was careful not to let her know that I was emotionally distressed. She looked at me with her eyes cast downward in sadness and asked if I would stay with her for a while. "Of course," I told her. I sat down on her bed and grabbed her hand. Together we watched the television with the volume so low it was almost silent. As usual it was the Disney Channel, her favorite. I continued to hold Sophie's hand until Peter got home. He peeked into her room to see what was happening. "Her head still hurts," I told him. I could see from the expression on his face that he was thinking, "Dammit, what is going on with my little girl?"

I realized that we all needed to eat some dinner so I made Sophie's favorite—macaroni and cheese. We all sat down together—Sophie, Peter, Casey, Molly, my mother Rochelle, and me—at the dining room table. She struggled to eat just a small portion, meanwhile trying to tell us that her head hurt, but no one was really paying attention. As Peter, Casey, and Molly sat laughing, I watched Sophie's facial expression take a downward turn. It was just a normal family dinner with lots of bantering, joking, and laughing, but this time it felt different for Sophie and I knew it. We weren't talking too loud, but the noise was pounding in her head as if she were at a rock concert.

When Sophie finally managed to tell everyone that they were too loud and that she couldn't take it, Peter, Casey, Molly, and her grandmother all looked at her and said okay, but then went on talking. They didn't mean to hurt Sophie but they really didn't understand what was happening to her. Sophie slowly raised her head and told us, with a defeated expression on her face, that she was going to bed. Then she looked straight at me. "Mom," she said, "I need you to come and stay with me." I said, quietly, "Of course I will stay with you." Off we went to her bedroom. I walked behind her, encouraging her to take a bath because I knew she found that soothing. Sophie just said, "No! I just need to go to bed." So I acquiesced, went into her room, and helped her get into her pajamas..

Sophie and I lay down together on her bed and I rubbed her head until she fell asleep. I watched her eyes slowly close and her face relax. The next thing I knew I was looking at Sophie's clock showing me that it was almost midnight, and I realized that I had fallen asleep next to her. Quietly, I rolled off the bed, desperate not to wake her up. Thank goodness she was sleeping. I walked groggily down the hall to my bed and got under the covers, pulling them over my head. I needed to feel protected from this awful thing that was happening to Sophie and to all of us. I lay there savoring the total quiet in the house and wondered whether I would ever know peace again. My daughter's pain had taken over all the quiet moments I had. But this was too much to ponder. At last, sleep came over me like a blanket and I escaped into the land of dreams.

I awoke the next morning to day three after Sophie's visit to the emergency room. I went to see how she was feeling. No surprise, she told me that she still had a headache. I told her that she did not have to go to school and she sighed with relief. There was no need to ask her whether she could do it. On her pale face was the expression of a sickly child at death's door. It was just too much for her to do anything. The nagging pain was making her a prisoner in her own body.

I told Sophie that she needed to stay with her grandmother that day as her father and I had to go to work. She looked disappointed that she would not have her mother by her side but I reminded her that we needed to go to work. She looked at me searchingly with sadness in her eyes but told me that she would be okay. I knew that she was telling me that to make me feel okay, but that it wasn't the truth. In fact, it was the furthest thing from the truth. I recognized that she wanted to make it okay for me and Peter. "She is so brave," I thought to myself.

Off to work I went, thinking that I would call Sophie during the day to find out how she was doing. On the way to work, Peter asked me what I thought was wrong with her and if she would be okay. He pounded away like a hammer with questions. I looked at him and answered truthfully, in an almost inaudible whisper, "I do not know."

Peter and I had discussed making an appointment for Sophie with the local pediatric neurologist. He told me he had called the neurologist and gotten an appointment for the following Tuesday morning at ten a.m. Hopefully, the neurologist would be able to determine what was wrong with Sophie and how to treat her problem. At least that is what I wanted to believe. A possible solution could be within reach, I told myself.

The next day, Sophie was unable to go to school once again. Peter and I discussed taking her to the pediatrician for a follow-up, which is what we were told to do at the hospital. Peter decided he would stay home and take Sophie to the doctor. I felt relieved that he was able to do this for our little girl. When I arrived at home, Peter told me that the pediatrician had recommended amoxicillin and had told him to see the neurologist as soon as possible. But why had they put her on amoxicillin? Peter was not clear on the exact reason, but said that he thought it had something to do with her blood work showing some kind of infection in her body. But Peter couldn't recall what it was about the blood work specifically. That made me angry. I never would have left the pediatrician's office until I was able to fully understand the exact reason for the antibiotic. I walked away to see Sophie, who asked me to help her go to sleep. I lay down with her and stayed close so I could comfort her. She told me that the pain had not gone away, and I ached deep within my psyche. I watched as her eyes began to close and sleep consumed her.

Now this is not the end.
It is not even the beginning
of the end. But it is, perhaps,
the end of the beginning.

—Winston Churchill

The Chiropractic Visit

The next morning Sophie still looked pale, but she reported that she felt slightly better and wanted to go to school in spite of her lingering headache. So I gave her some Motrin to help with the pain and took her to school late. A couple of hours later I got a call from the nurse who told me that Sophie's head was hurting really badly. After only a couple of hours for her at school and me at work, I left work to pick her up and take her home once again.

Sophie looked so pale and limp when I saw her. She got her backpack and it was as if she were moving in slow motion while walking toward me. I put my arm around her and together we slowly walked out to the car. Sophie had an air of defeat encompassing her. I got into the car with a sigh of relief. Wondering if I should take her to my chiropractor, I asked, "Sophie would you go with me to see the chiropractor?" She looked at me, dog-tired, and in a tiny mouse voice, said, "Okay mom."

I stared at her in the rearview mirror and began driving in the direction of the chiropractor's office. It was only about ten minutes from the school. When we walked into the waiting area, the receptionist looked at Sophie and said, "You don't look like you are feeling well today." Sophie shrugged and said, "No." Then the receptionist looked back at me with a face that told me that Sophie looked really awful. I shook my head and gave her a knowing look. We sat down next to each other to wait for Dr. Mark Goldhirsch. Sophie leaned against my shoulder and told me in a low voice that her head still hurt. What could I do to take away the pain? I tried to comfort her by telling her that maybe the chiropractor would be able to help us. She looked up at me and said, "Mom, I know you want to help me, but I am not sure that anyone can." I could never have imagined that the pain could get any worse. Just then the chiropractor exited his adjustment room and waved at us to enter. He looked at Sophie and agreed with me that her face had a pale, pasty color to it. He suggested doing kinesiology (muscle testing) on her to determine what was going on inside of her. So he went through the steps and was able to identify a bacterium in her body, but was unable to determine the specific type of bacteria.

He asked how it all started, so I told him about the cough, the headaches, and the sound sensitivity. He told me that his son had Lyme disease as a very young child and that he and his wife had taken him to see an infectious disease specialist in Albany. He then offered some homeopathic medicine that the muscle testing had shown Sophie would respond to, and suggested that an infectious disease specialist might be able to identify what bacteria was inside her body. "Okay," I said. "We will give this a try." We left the office with the homeopathic medicine.

As we got into the car, I could see from Sophie's expression that she felt she was losing the battle. I hoped that the homeopathic medicine would help. I knew she would need something more than just homeopathic treatment, but right now any medicine would do. In fact, I was beginning to realize, she probably would need more than just one medication to get well.

However, I was determined not to let what was happening to my little girl crush me. I was going to keep on searching until I found the doctor and medications that would help her. But in the meantime, I felt lost and terribly powerless. I was traveling down a road that was so unfamiliar to me. Did I have the skills to help find a way to get my daughter well? Did a path to wellness even exist?

Each and every moment of my day was filled with worry, stemming from the constant, vivid observation that my child was suffering. She was being tormented by an invisible monster that could not be identified by the doctors. I felt as if I were the only way to her salvation, yet I also felt hopelessly powerless. The realization that I might not be able to fix my child hit me like a ton of bricks. And then I realized that maybe the doctors would not be able to fix her either.

I wondered how I would manage emotionally to get through the weekend, and how I would cope over the next few days until the visit with the neurologist. Would I be able to handle the fact that she needed me every waking moment to be at her side? Sophie had let me know that's what she needed, and there was no way that I would let her down. Fear and dread followed her like a dark cloud and made her unable to be alone. We just had to survive the weekend, hoping that there would be answers on Tuesday.

Back home, I tried to make the house as quiet as possible for my little girl. Noise caused a stabbing pain in her eardrums. She looked like she was in agony whenever the noise level at home reached a volume that only she heard as excruciating.

Fortunately, we survived the weekend, which ended with the pain in Sophie's head having lessened, but still moving around inside her skull.

Believing in progress does
not mean believing that any
progress has yet been made.

—Franz Kafka

It was Monday morning, the day before the neurology
visit, and Sophie was still not well. She got dressed and
came into our bedroom complaining of blurry vision. I
asked her, "What do you mean?" She told me that her
eyes were blurry and the vision came and went. "How
long has this been happening?" I asked her. She said it
had just started that morning and it was scaring her. She
thought she had gone blind for a minute as well.

I quickly decided that she was not well enough
to attend school. So there we were with another frightening symptom to add to the list. I was more anxious than
ever to get her to the neurologist. "Please," I thought,
"let this day pass quickly."

Tuesday morning arrived, but not quickly enough, and off we went to the neurologist. Sophie's father accompanied us. She still looked pale and struggled to get herself together, the whole time looking sadly at us, her mother and father, as if she were imploring us to take the awful pain in her head away. "Mommy," she said, "my head still hurts." I told her with as much confidence as I could muster that the neurologist would figure out what to do about her headaches.

Sophie stared at me, trying hard to believe me. I felt like a liar, as if I were selling my own child a line of false nonsense. How could I tell her that I didn't really know if the neurologist would be able to help her, that I only hoped so? How could I tell her that she might come away from the visit and still be in pain with no relief in sight? My heart leapt into my throat and tears filled my eyes. How could this be happening? In my head, I was screaming this mantra over and over again. But somehow I maintained a calm demeanor, as if I were in total control. Nobody could glimpse my agony.

Peter drove us to the neurologist's office in silence. We wanted to speak but there were no words that could make any of us feel better. Even though we were trying to act like this was a routine visit, there was nothing routine about what was happening. The inevitable truth was that we knew nothing about what was happening to our daughter—and the doctors didn't know either. I felt stuck with no answers, stuck with her pain. I just wanted her to get some relief. Was there anyone out there who could help my daughter? In my mind I was yelling, "Help, I need help, my daughter needs help!"

We arrived at the neurologist's office and I got out of the car and walked around to Sophie's side, opened the door, and reached for her hand. Holding her arm, with her body closely aligned with mine, we began walking slowly up the steps to the building. Each step was an effort for Sophie. This made me realize that movement just kept her pain going, as if an electric current ran right through her and we had no access to the switch that could turn it off. We walked through the glass, steel framed doors. Peter held open the door to the waiting area as we walked inside. Then the three of us sat and waited, staring into the open space of the waiting area until Peter's cell phone buzzed and he was up and pacing, talking business. I looked at Sophie and squeezed her hand, attempting to give her some nonverbal reassurance. Soon we got called into the exam room. A computer screen sat on a counter waiting to log in the next patient, my daughter. I helped Sophie onto the exam table but then she held me close, not wanting to let me go. It was still morning and already I felt exhausted. I stood next to my daughter as she moaned softly with pain. A sudden urge to pace the room was gnawing at me, but I stood still, holding her in a cocoon of my arms. My adrenaline continued pushing me to move, but I was unable to pull apart from Sophie. I took a deep breath of air, hoping it would calm me. My fear was a vibration that sent chills throughout my body, as if a tarantula had bitten me and its venom was spreading through me. I woke up from my reverie of dreadful imaginings when a woman entered the room and introduced herself as the Nurse Practitioner. She sat down in a chair near the computer screen and began the routine questioning of what had led up to this visit.

"So when did the headaches begin?" she asked. I began to tell the tale of the symptoms Sophie had been experi-

encing—from the headaches that seemed at first episodic until the most recent headache that had been ongoing
for about four days. I went on to explain how Sophie
had never been sick with any recurring symptoms. "She
had always been a healthy child," I said. After all the
pertinent questions had been answered, the nurse asked
if Sophie ever had a tick bite. "Yes," I told her. "Sophie
had a tick bite in 2008 and another one in 2009, about
six months ago."

The tick bite in 2008 was on the back of Sophie's head
and the hairdresser discovered it. I removed the tick myself. The tick bite in 2009 was on Sophie's shoulder, and
I also removed that tick myself. The nurse practitioner
nodded. Had the hospital taken a Lyme test at our most
recent visit to the emergency room? "Yes," I said. "The
doctor asked about a tick bite and the hospital staff took
a Lyme test, but the doctor said there were no significant
findings from the test." The nurse practitioner told me
that she was going to request the results of the test immediately. As she got up to leave the room, I asked, "Do
you think it is Lyme?" She looked at me and said, "It
sounds like Lyme, but let me get the results of the test."

After she left the exam room, Peter got another call
and told me that he needed to leave. I looked at him and
said, "I've got it, go." He asked whether I could handle
it without him. I said, "It's okay, just go." Frustration
had begun to erupt inside of me. It appeared to me that
he was indifferent to our daughter's medical dilemma.
Work was luring him away from us. He walked over to
Sophie and kissed her forehead, asking her if she would
be okay. She stared at him with a look of annoyance and
told him, "Dad, just go." He turned away and out the
door he went. My daughter Molly was going to pick us

up from the neurologist's office so we could get home. I texted her and she replied, "I'm on my way." Thank goodness she was there to help.

Then it was just Sophie and I, together, waiting. Sophie looked at me impatiently. She couldn't wait until this doctor visit was over. Her pain was continuous. I sat still, right next to her, holding her hand as she moaned and looked at me for answers. I whispered to her that I would get her the help she needed even if this doctor did not have the answer. "I will not stop until I find the doctor that will help you," I told her, "and you should never forget that."

"I know, Mom," she said. "I know."

The nurse practitioner came back into the room and asked whether we had seen the doctor yet. I shook my head no. She told us that she received the results of the Lyme test and that the Elisa test was reactive, but the Western Blot test was negative. She went on to say that even though the Western Blot test showed one positive band, #41, the doctor would probably tell us that she did not have Lyme disease. I was totally lost as to what all this meant. Was the band #41 significant? She tried to explain to me that if the test results were not positive, most doctors would say it was not Lyme disease. What was defined as positive? Could she still have Lyme disease with one positive band? I was confounded by the tests and how they were interpreted. I figured when I got home I would look up the tests and try to figure out what they meant. As the nurse practitioner and I were talking, the neurologist walked in. He seemed like a friendly man and introduced himself with enthusiasm. Once again, I went over the story, synopsizing all the symptoms my daughter had been experiencing: excruciating headaches that wouldn't let up, blurry vision, and extreme sensitivity to sound were the primary complaints. I also recounted the visit to the pediatrician and how the doctor there put her on amoxicillin after the emergency room visit. "Why she was put on amoxicillin?" the neurologist asked. I didn't know how to respond. All I could say was that Sophie's father had taken her to the pediatrician as recommended by the ER doctors. The pediatrician had not clearly explained why he put her on amoxicillin.

The neurologist proceeded with the routine neurological exam as I sat and observed. When he had finished, I recall him saying, "There is no neurological problem here." He turned to the nurse practitioner to look at the results of the Lyme test, looked me straight in the eye, and, as I recall, he stated, "I believe it is Lyme disease."

At last we had a diagnosis. But did that mean we had made progress? I didn't really feel very confident about the diagnosis because I knew absolutely nothing about Lyme disease.

The neurologist confidently told me to keep Sophie on the amoxicillin and he gave me another prescription with the instructions to return in two weeks. What else could I do? I had to trust this neurologist and go with the diagnosis and his recommendation. And I now had to start to learn about Lyme disease.

Would the amoxicillin work for Sophie? I had no knowledge of the complexity of Lyme disease and the co-infections that often accompany it. I was lacking in knowledge of how the treatment was doled out and afraid that I would be facing a losing battle when it came to understanding Lyme disease.

After the doctor visit, Sophie and I left the neurologist's office to go home to rest. I felt exhausted. Sophie was having a rough time with the symptoms she had been experiencing and struggled to cope with the changing symptoms picture. We lay down together on her bed so I could comfort her. I had become her security blanket but was unable to bring her to safety. Together we watched the Disney Channel, Nickelodeon, and the Family Channel. Sophie told me that watching television took her mind off what was happening to her, at least for short periods of time. But fear was written across her face. The pain she suffered was evident in every movement she made. It was not possible to locate the words necessary to describe the pain she was feeling. I knew that she needed me to be physically close to her as much as possible. I was going to try and be there for her as much as I could since I still had to work. We got through the next couple of days, but she did not seem to be getting any better—in fact, she looked even paler and weaker. She continued to complain about the headache not going away, but we hoped that it would get better even if progress was slow.

If you don't know where you are going, any road will get you there.

—Lewis Carroll

The Nurse Practitioner

On the following Saturday, I was at work when all of the sudden I got a phone call from Peter. He was frantic.

"Mindy, you have got to come home immediately."

"What's wrong?"

"Sophie can't walk."

"What?"

"I told you, Sophie can't walk."

I asked him what had happened without fully absorbing what he just told me. He said it again, "She can't walk, I'm telling you, she can't walk!" For a moment I was stunned. Then I tried to gather my thoughts. I explained that he must get her in the car and take her to the pediatrician's office where I would meet him.

I canceled my appointments for the rest of the day, packed up, and left my office. In my car, I was moving so quickly in and out of traffic that I felt like a race car driver. There weren't many vehicles on the road, but that didn't matter because all I could hear was the sound of my breathing, my adrenaline flowing, and my heart pumping. I was unable to think because I was so overwhelmed with what Peter had told me. He could get a little frantic sometimes, but I knew what he had told me was true even though I did not want to believe it. How could I believe that my daughter was suddenly unable to walk? How could something like that happen overnight? It was as if my mind had been pushed out of the airplane of life, and was falling to the ground with no parachute. There was no safety net in this situation.

Finally, I reached the pediatrician's office. I quickly got out of the car and ran, huffing and puffing, up the stairs into the building. Once again, it was the adrenaline pumping through my veins that gave me the surge of energy to move quickly. Anxiety was running through me like electricity. "I am looking for my daughter, Sophie, who just arrived," I told the front desk. The woman behind the desk looked up at me and, seeing a frantic, out-of-breath mother, told me without further delay that my daughter was downstairs. I turned and rushed down the stairs and walked into the exam room to see Sophie sitting in a wheelchair, pale as a ghost.

I stared, shocked, then noticed Peter and the nurse practitioner standing there looking at me. "What happened?" I asked. Peter told me again that Sophie was unable to walk. I looked at the nurse practitioner and she calmly looked back at me. "What are we supposed to do now?" I asked. She told us that Sophie's vitals were normal but that she looked pale and sickly. I queried her about whether this was connected to Lyme disease and discussed what the neurologist had stated to me. She said it could be Lyme disease, but that she could not say for sure. She seemed genuinely concerned for our daughter and told us that she thought Sophie should be admitted into the hospital. We discussed the possibilities of where to go—locally or farther away. After some discussion, we chose the farther away hospital, hoping there would be answers for our daughter and her illness. The nurse practitioner told us that she would call the emergency room to let them know we would be coming.

Sophie asked to ride with me, so I told her that was okay. Peter agreed that Sophie should ride with me and he would follow in his car. "Okay, I guess we have a plan," I said. Together we helped Sophie out of the wheelchair. I held her in my arms and slowly walked up the stairs, out the door, and to my car with Peter right behind me.

The true triumph of reason is that it enables us to get along with those who do not possess it.

—Voltaire

The Emergency Room

About two hours later, we arrived at the hospital. We went through the emergency room as the nurse practitioner had suggested. After giving the detailed information to the patient registration representative, I asked him whether the nurse practitioner from the pediatric group had called to provide any information along with her recommendation that we take Sophie to the hospital. He explained that he would need to check that, and made a phone call as I stood and waited. When he was off the phone, he told me that she had called. I falsely assumed that this information would provide what was needed for my daughter to be admitted into the hospital, and we all took seats in the waiting area while Sophie complained of pains in her legs. "It hurts," she told me. "It really hurts." I tried to reassure her by saying that we were in the hospital and that we would find out what was wrong with her. I tried to make her feel safe in the hospital. I spoke from the heart in my feeble attempt to comfort her. I really wanted to believe that we would find the answers at the hospital. The outcome was still mysterious to me.

I continued to tell her to be patient, but there was agony in her eyes. She was hurting, really hurting. The pain in her legs started to get worse. She pointed to her shins and told me she felt like someone was stabbing her. I talked to her as if I understood what was happening, but that was not even close to the truth. I tried to convince her that I knew we would be able to solve this puzzle. I took her hand in mine and squeezed it, looking straight into her eyes. I said, "I am here with you and we will find out what is wrong." I promised her, as I truly believed that I would find out what was hurting my baby girl, even though I was unable to verify this claim.

After an hour had passed, Sophie let out soft moans because of the pain. Then two hours had passed, and just as I was about to ask what was going on, a nurse entered the waiting area and called Sophie's name. She directed us through two large, electric doors into the inner sanctum of the hospital emergency area, where you get a bed with a curtain. Sophie's bed was by a window. I looked out the window into the darkness of night. Only the hospital lights glared back at me. Would there be answers? I took a deep breath, then turned around to face my daughter's pain.

Together, Peter and I sat down on either side of Sophie. We looked at her small, pale, forlorn face and listened to her moaning. The pain in her legs would not let up. We continued to wait. Our patience was on a short fuse. A doctor came in to check on Sophie, performing the traditional neurological examination. He checked her reflexes, trying to identify the source of her illness and its location. No such luck it seemed, and without a word, the doctor left the curtained room. I stood, staring at the path he took out of Sophie's curtained off room. Just take a deep breath, I told myself. Three hours had passed and the pain was intensifying. Sophie's moaning was continuous now. Again, she told us she felt like something was stabbing her legs, but the pain had now traveled to her ankles. I tried to understand what was happening to her and asked her if there was any way she could explain the pain. She said she felt as if she were being beaten with a baseball bat. I was left with a picture that I could not get out my head.

By the fourth hour in the ER Sophie was making so much noise that it was disturbing the other patients in their curtained-off beds. An intern came in to check on her and told her that she must quiet down. Peter and I stared at him. Quiet down? I felt exasperated. Had he not been listening for the last four hours to what had been happening to my daughter? I felt an intense anger welling up inside of me, but my anger, like me, had nowhere to go. I felt trapped by my own ignorance. There I was, at the lowest, most helpless moment in my life, succumbing to the voice of authority, a doctor intern. And I was soon to discover just how little authority I had over my daughter in this hospital.

By the fifth hour, Sophie was still moaning. The sound of her pain was getting louder. By now she had had at least six neurological exams by doctors and doctor interns. When another intern arrived to perform yet another neurological exam, I thought to myself, "You have got to be kidding me. Have you not heard her all this time in pain?" The doctor asked her to sit up. She was unable to sit up without help so Peter and I helped her to sit up. In a robotic manner, the intern went through the motions of the neurological exam. "Can you give her something for the pain?" I asked. His reply was cold and unfeeling, and I recall him saying, "Let me see, I am an intern and I need to speak with the ER doctor." Helplessly, I replied, "Okay." So we waited some more.

By the sixth hour, I needed a break. I decided to walk outside to get some fresh air. I was hoping that the cold would numb me and take away my feeling of helplessness. It was a crisp night in March. I took in cold breaths of air as I walked around in a circle. Then I walked back in through the electronic doors into the inner sanctum and watched the interns sitting behind a long counter covered with computer screens, chatting and laughing as if they were sitting together in a coffee bar without a care in the world. I stood there for a long moment, watching and waiting, but not one of them looked up at me or asked me if I wanted or needed anything. In my despair, I said out loud, "Excuse me." A few heads turned my way. I go on, "Can someone give my daughter something for the pain?" Finally, I had them trapped, and there was a pause in their conversation. I stood and stared at them, waiting for a response. "Someone will be with you shortly," one of them finally replied. I glared at them, wishing I could burn a hole right through each and every one of them to make them know the pain my daughter was enduring right next door.

But I could see that my attempt to connect was going largely unnoticed, so I walked back to the curtained room where Sophie was. By then she was screaming in pain, pointing to her legs: "Mommy it hurts really bad! Ahhhhhhhhhhhhhhhhhhhhhhhhhhhhhhhhhhhhhhhhhhh-hhhh!" Finally, one of the interns came into the room to explain that he had talked with the doctor and was getting ready to give her something for the pain. Hallelujah! "What are you going to give her?" I asked. The intern replied, "The doctor said to give her Toradol [a pain killer]."

The intern put in a peripherally inserted central catheter, a form of intravenous access that can be used for a prolonged period of time, and gave her a drip, so Peter and I assumed that now she would get some relief. The intern explained that she should feel better soon, but another hour passed with no pain reduction in sight. By then, the seventh hour had come and gone. Again, I went outside of the curtained room to watch the interns chatting away together. I stood waiting and watching for a moment and then felt fed up. "Excuse me," I said. "The medication you gave my daughter isn't doing anything for her." Again, they looked toward me. One of the interns got up and came over to me. "So what can you give her to help the pain?" I asked. The intern told me that she would be in the room momentarily.

Frustrated, I went back to Sophie, who was exhausted and drained, just like Peter and I. More time passed and we moved into our eighth hour there. The intern suddenly rushed into the room, explaining that the doctor had recommended a pediatric dose of morphine. I didn't know whether to be shocked, frightened, or relieved. Morphine sounded so extreme, so strong, like it was the last straw, the last intervention. So my nine-year-old daughter was going to be given a pediatric dose of morphine. I felt terrified but was still hoping that this would give my daughter some relief, so I acquiesced to the hospital's recommendation. The intern got the medication and walked into the room, all businesslike, to connect the medication to the PICC line. We watched as the medication poured effortlessly into her body through the drip line. We stood watching our daughter, waiting for something to happen, hoping that her eyelids would close as she drifted off to sleep. We continued to watch and wait, but there was no land of sleep calling to her. She screamed in pain. Peter and I tried to comfort her but it was no use. It was as if we were experiencing an earthquake. The ground was crackling beneath our feet and we were going to be sucked down into an abyss.

When the ninth hour arrived, the doctor on duty came in. It was just past midnight, and I recall the doctor saying, "Well, I guess you can't take her home like this. We will get a room ready for her." I stood looking at the doctor. How could he say that to me so nonchalantly? I guess you can't take her home like this. What did he mean? Was he acknowledging that she was in fact sick by arranging a room for her in the hospital?

I continued to stare at this person, relieved but in disbelief. "We will let you know when the room is ready," he said. "It shouldn't take very long." A deep sigh reverberated inside me as I told my little girl that she was being admitted to the hospital. I explained that we were waiting for them to get a room ready for her. The whole time, I was holding Sophie's hand and squeezing it to say the unspoken words of love, encouragement, and hope.

Finally, Sophie was quietly taken upstairs to a room with a view and settled into a hospital bed. Would we ever be given a medical explanation for Sophie's circumstances? This type of thinking started to scare the crap out of me.

Apparently, there is nothing that can happen today.

—Mark Twain

The Hospital Stay–Day One

In Sophie's room there was a small sofa covered with a thick vinyl material that pulled out into a small double bed. The nurse provided sheets, a pillow, and a blanket for the pull-out so that Peter and I could stay with her overnight. There was a comforting feeling in the children's unit. The nurse's station was right outside the door. The walkways were covered in carpet, probably to keep the area quiet. It was a relief to be there.

The tiredness was creeping up my spine. I was ready to collapse on any piece of furniture in the hospital that I could locate to lay my weary body. I told Peter that I would stay, and directed him to go home. "One of us needs a good night's rest," I said. He nodded, walked over to Sophie, kissed her forehead, and walked out the door of her room. Sophie fell asleep rather quickly, but I tossed and turned on the sofa bed, trying to unwind, my mind on overdrive. Somehow, I was finally able to fall asleep.

The next morning arrived. The breakfast was not what Sophie hoped for so she requested some cold cereal. I helped her get up, go to the bathroom, wash her face, and brush her teeth. She was unable to stand without my help. If I let her try to walk on her own and she had nothing to lean against for support she would collapse onto the floor. After assisting her with this semblance of a daily routine, I got her positioned comfortably in the hospital bed. Sophie wanted to watch television so I turned it on. The distraction helped to calm her fears, but she still complained of pain in her legs. I could see that she was trying her best to deal with the pain, but it was sucking out every bit of happiness she had ever seen, felt, or experienced. There was nothing left for her to enjoy except the distraction of the television.

Around mid-morning, the doctor came into the room and introduced herself. She began to talk to Sophie and I by asking some questions while reviewing the details of how Sophie had wound up in the hospital. We told her about the symptoms once again—the headaches, blurry vision, knee pain, shin pain, ankle pain, sound sensitivity, and, of course, the foremost tragedy, not being able to walk. I told her that the outpatient pediatric neurologist had said it was Lyme disease, but she did not respond to what I was saying. Instead, she went on checking Sophie's reflexes. She totally ignored what I had reported to her regarding what the neurologist had stated to me. It was as if Lyme disease did not exist.

Was there any medical person in this hospital able to do anything but a neurological exam? It was so frustrating to watch my daughter being subjected to the same exam over and over again with the same results. She couldn't walk. Was it so difficult to process that fact? What were these doctors thinking?

Finally, the doctor told us that a neurologist would be in later to see Sophie. Then she asked Sophie some direct questions. Sophie repeated the tale and told the doctor what was happening to her. She tried to describe the pain in her legs, which wouldn't let up, and how she was unable to walk. Yet each doctor that arrived tried to get her to stand up and take a few steps, as if by some miracle she would suddenly start walking after all. Sophie was trying so hard to attempt to walk, but as soon as each doctor let go of her elbow, she collapsed to the floor. Why did they keep trying to get her to walk? She had just told the doctor that she was in pain, so why wouldn't the doctor listen? Why weren't any of the doctors listening?

I watched what was happening between Sophie and the doctors like a helpless observer to a robbery. Each one tried to get her to walk until she collapsed onto the floor. Then each doctor would look at her on the floor and lean down to help her get up and back onto the bed. It was quite maddening to watch this episode over and over again. The latest doctor instructed the nurse to check Sophie's vitals, then ordered the nurse to put Sophie on a Motrin drip for her pain, to be given every eight hours. I felt as if I were being robbed of my motherhood. There I stood, but I was not being asked for my opinion or whether I even thought it was okay to give my daughter the eight-hour Motrin drip. Nevertheless, I stood there feeling powerless. Had I lost my power as a mother? Had I given up and handed my daughter over to these nurses and doctors?

Like a robot, the nurse left and came back with the equipment to take her vitals, but didn't report any of it to me. She then gave Sophie Motrin without even asking her how she was feeling. I felt invisible, as if I had died and returned as a ghost, watching my daughter struggle but unable to communicate with her or help her. There seemed to be only one side—the hospital's side. Was I a visitor in my own life? I was able to see others walking in and out of my life, but they were unable to see me. While I sat by her side making every effort to comfort her, they only saw Sophie.

Finally the room was empty except for Sophie and me. I held her hand and she struggled to smile, but I knew it was a pretend smile. It was nothing more than a feeble attempt to encourage hope, but it was a hope that felt so far away it could not be touched. Sophie's smile was a crooked one that disappeared from her face whenever I turned my head.

The television created a sound barrier so words didn't have to be spoken. Sophie looked up at the screen with a blank stare. It was soon lunchtime, and once again Sophie was disappointed in the food. She requested the substitute, a peanut-butter-and-jelly sandwich. Somewhat satisfied with her choice, she slowly took a few bites while looking at the television. I sat back on the vinyl sofa and stared into space. I felt a bit exhausted so I jumped up to go locate a distraction. Sophie tried to sit up and said, "Mom, where are you going?" There was fear in her voice. "Nowhere," I replied. "Nowhere." I stood in the doorway, looking around at anything outside of the room. My eyes roamed the hallway as if I were channel surfing. There was a terrible, empty feeling inside me. I turned around and walked right back into the room. I asked Sophie if she needed anything and she told me that she didn't, so I went to the vinyl sofa and plopped down to try to read the newspaper, but the words I read were all meaningless.

Then, all of the sudden, a gray-haired man in a suit walked into the room and introduced himself as the neurologist. He stated his name and seemed genuinely interested in Sophie's case. Once again, the neurological exam began. Sophie was doing just fine until he asked her to walk. While she was trying to pull her head up from the pillow and turn her body to one side of the bed, he continued to ask questions about what had happened. Sophie answered, and then I did, and back and forth we went, reiterating the tale of how it all began. He listened attentively to the details of the story. At times he even stopped the exam to pay attention to what either Sophie or I was saying to him. He finally asked her to sit at the edge of the bed. Slowly, she moved herself as best she could to the edge of the bed and sat with her legs dangling toward the floor. He held her arm at the elbow and helped her to stand up. She was able to stand as long as she was leaning on his arm. Then he told her to try and take a step. She tried, being the kind of child who does not want to disappoint people, but she was unable to hold herself up so she leaned against the doctor. He told her to sit back down on the bed.

The neurologist looked perplexed, but behaved in a cordial manner. As I recall the conversation, he reported, "I do not see any neurological problems." Then he went on to explain to us that there would be other tests to determine what was happening. He tried to reassure us, informing us with the routine hospital monologue of more tests. I nodded in agreement, as if I were totally on board with what he was telling me. I was a novice in the game of search and identify what is wrong with the body. Nighttime arrived. Maybe we could get some sleep. I wished I would wake up from this nightmare that had descended upon my family, but there was not a chance of that happening for me, my intuition told me, not a chance. Day One in the hospital was now over with nothing to show for it.

We must accept finite
disappointment, but never
lose infinite hope.

—Martin Luther King, Jr.

The next morning came so quickly that when I awakened it did not feel like I had slept at all. I felt as if a brick was attached to each of my feet as I got up to go to the bathroom. Like steel posts, my legs moved slowly, bending slightly as if I were in a hypnotic trance.

Day Two had arrived, and what would it bring? Thoughts were floating around in my head but I was unable to make sense of what was happening around me. Breakfast quickly went from the table straight into the garbage. Sophie was still dissatisfied with the tasteless food … and was still unable to walk by herself. As the late morning arrived, a woman walked into the room and put her hand out to shake mine. She introduced herself as the psychiatrist and began with an array of questions about what had happened to Sophie. All over again, I recited the story from the beginning up until the present, trying not to leave out the essential points along the way. The psychiatrist nodded as if she was listening attentively to the story. As I came to the end of the tale of woe, she asked some questions about Sophie regarding her mental state and physical symptoms. Then she proceeded to query me on Sophie's developmental history and any recent stressors. Within twenty minutes, she seemed satisfied with the data she had collected. The final remarks verbally noted by the psychiatrist before she left the room were that Sophie had a supportive family and there did not seem to be any current stressors. I was grateful that the assessments were being completed. I saw no need to worry about the mental status exam performed by the psychiatrist because I believed that Sophie had a medical condition yet to be identified.

The daily report by the medical staff indicated leg weakness and gait difficulties. The Motrin was being given on schedule without consulting Sophie or me. The nurse was infusing the automatic drip every eight hours. Next, Sophie's blood was taken for analysis. The results yielded more questions about whether she'd had a recent strep infection. I indicated that she had had strep in the past but that I could not recall exactly when. Apparently, something in the blood analysis revealed a recent strep infection. Of course, there were other diagnoses being considered, one of which was chorea. The reason this diagnosis was being considered by the neurologist was because Sophie had some involuntary movement of her hands. When the neurologist tried to get Sophie to stand during his visit, her hands started shaking. Chorea is an abnormal, involuntary movement disorder caused by over-activity of the neurotransmitter dopamine in the areas of the brain that control movement. However, in the end, Sophie did not have enough of the symptoms to be diagnosed with this condition.

Next, the doctors decided to put her on penicillin, thinking that maybe the strep infection had not been resolved. I recall being told that this was a prophylactic measure—a preventive intervention for what, I was not sure. There was no doctor to say confidently whether it was absolutely necessary to put her on the penicillin or if it would do anything for her. Instead, they were going to proceed with this antibiotic just in case. But was this an answer? I felt adrenaline begin to rush through my body again. I felt enraged one moment and defeated the next.

Everything was being done according to the premise that a preventative measure was necessary. Were these doctors at work thinking that they were preventing the possibility of a disease that might be lurking inside of my daughter's helpless body? Was there some kind of guessing game going on by these professionals because no one wanted to appear to be an inadequate medical expert? Or was it that they needed some kind of diagnosis to hang their hat on for insurance reimbursement? I knew that something was really wrong with my daughter. As she lay there in the hospital bed, I could see that she was getting sicker and sicker. Yet not one doctor had a clue what to do. They were lost and could not admit it, but I had to stay there and allow them to complete the testing. I was still hoping that even just a tiny, single dot of knowledge would emerge, revealing a clue as to what was happening to my little girl.

Hope is a waking Dream.

—Aristotle

Day Three began with the administration of medication waking Sophie earlier than usual. The dawn light was seeping through the window. I lay on the pullout sofa watching the nurse wake my daughter to give her Motrin for her pain. Nothing had changed except for the promise of more tests. The neurologist had visited Sophie the night before to provide the same neurological exam yet again, and then tried to get her to walk. She was being studied like a caged animal, poked and prodded by the hands of doctors. How could I watch this over and over again?

Doctors came and went without giving me any information as they looked at my daughter and asked superfluous questions. On and on they went as if she were an experimental patient that they couldn't wait to get their hands on to do what they pleased. They all had the pompous confidence of medical experts but they couldn't locate the foundation of Sophie's illness. The hospital staff's grandiosity had taken over and I was still invisible to them. How could I sit in the hospital, mindless, feeling like my brain had lost its satellite connection? All we could do was wait, wait, and wait some more. Sophie was watching television. How could I tell her that the doctors didn't know what was wrong with her? I felt as if I had been deceived. All I wanted was to promise my little girl some hope—just an ounce of hope would be the best medicine she could get.

There are only two ways to live your life. One is as though nothing is a miracle. The other is as though everything is a miracle.

—Albert Einstein

For better or worse the fourth day had arrived. The doctor and the neurologist began ordering the tests. An MRI of Sophie's brain would be one of them as well as an MRI of her spine. That day the psychologist was also scheduled to see Sophie. After four straight days in the hospital watching Sophie lay there in bed, watching the nurses come and go, taking her vitals, providing her comfort with the continuing Motrin drip and the penicillin, I had to go home and take a break. Finally, there would be a break in the nightmare of my life. Peter would be taking over this afternoon, and so after his arrival, I left the hospital. Limping my way to the car with the life half sucked out of my gut, I got on the road home.

I called my middle daughter, Molly, and asked if she wanted to have lunch with me the following day. "Of course," she replied with enthusiasm. Unfortunately, I was unable to respond back with an ounce of joy. I felt bad, really bad that I could not give her more of me. I had become a desolate street in the lives of my other children. That was the way I felt most of the time: mentally and emotionally drained. I was just a big hole that needed to get filled with answers.

The following day, Molly and I met at a local restaurant in town. She was really happy to be alone with me and told me so. It was hard for her to see me giving everything I had to Sophie and only leaving an empty plate for her when she was emotionally hungry. She was hungry for my time and my attention, hungry to share her thoughts with me, be with me, laugh with me, and have me be her mom. The mom she had known all her life had disappeared because of Sophie's illness. Molly understood why it had to be this way but she did not like it. I was trying my hardest to reach out to her and connect with her with what little of me I had left to share. Even though Sophie's illness had become the focus for everyone in our family, Molly was still my other little girl, and I needed to try my hardest to let her know it. However, the reality of Sophie's situation was becoming clearer to me: We would be in the dark far longer than I had anticipated.

While Molly and I were chatting and ordering our food, a family friend sitting at another table nearby asked me how Sophie was doing. I told him she was in the hospital and I believed the cause was Lyme disease. I had never said it out loud until that moment. It was then that I realized my belief, the belief that my daughter had Lyme disease. Our friend answered back that he was sorry to hear that and hoped that she would be getting better soon. As we were talking, I noticed a woman sitting alone nearby eating her lunch, listening attentively to our conversation. I am not sure what drew her attention to us, but she was concentrating hard on what we were saying. I made nothing of it and after a brief back-and-forth, I returned my attention to Molly and our conversation. Molly was relieved to have me all to herself but was worried about her sister and how this situation was creating a blanket of sadness over our family—a blanket that was beginning to suffocate us with a feeling of doom.

Our food arrived. As Molly and I began to dig in and eat, the woman who was previously listening attentively to my conversation with the family friend walked over to our table. She quickly introduced herself as Marilyn. In a daze, I looked up at her and listened. She went on to write the name of a doctor on the back of an appointment card and hand it to me, and looking me straight in the eye, told me in a soft and gentle voice, "You call this doctor and he will help you." Astonished, I gratefully took the card and examined it like it was a precious jewel in my hand. The name on the card was Dr. Daniel Cameron. I placed it in my purse for safekeeping. This was a card I did not want to lose.

For a few moments I was stunned. My daughter watched me and then tried to reengage in our previous conversation. But I could not go back there. I had to talk about the woman, the card, and the doctor's name, as if a miracle had just occurred. It was indeed a miracle that had just taken place. This woman was an angel and she had come to assist me, to answer my prayer.

That evening when I got home I began my own research regarding Lyme disease. I sat down at the computer and started with Google, reading whatever I could find about Lyme disease. I needed to know everything I could find on the Internet. What I discovered assured me without a doubt that Sophie was suffering the symptoms of Lyme disease. Blurry vision, headaches, shooting pains in the legs, shins, knees, and ankles, and sensitivity to sound were all identified as major symptoms of Lyme disease, and Sophie had them all.

On the Center for Disease Control website, fever, headache, fatigue, and a characteristic rash called erythema migrans were all identified as the primary symptoms of Lyme disease. It further indicated that if left untreated, the bacteria could spread to the joints, the heart, and the nervous system.

My head was spinning with information, so I decided to take a bath and relax. I was so exhausted that when I got out of the tub all I could do was lie down. My head was sinking into the pillow as I turned on the television to channel surf. I did not want to hear the thoughts in my head, and the noise of the television successfully blocked them for me. It was a worthy distraction until my eyelids grew heavy. Finally, my eyes closed for the night. Nothing was visible but the empty space of a black hole.

The only true wisdom is knowing you know nothing.

—Socrates

The Hospital Stay–Day Five

It was another morning, Day Five in the hospital, but I had to go to work. I would return to the hospital that evening. For just a moment that morning I felt as if everything had been as it was before Sophie got ill. I scanned the bedroom and felt a momentary peacefulness, but a split second later my mind took me back to reality. I tried to pull myself out of bed but my body felt like lead. How could this be happening to me? My thoughts had marched like an intruder right through my head without regard for my sanity. Was there any sanity to be had with my child lying in a hospital without a diagnosis? I thought not. But I had to get to work—that would help me take my mind off Sophie's predicament for a little while longer. I rushed to shower, get dressed, and give my face some color with a spattering of makeup.

As always, I was in a rush as I dashed out to the car, anticipating what would be happening at work. I arrived without an emergency call. Hallelujah! All day long I watched the clock like a prisoner waiting for my release so I could travel to the hospital where I would enter the prison that was my child's illness. At last, the workday was over, and without hesitation I got into my car. I started driving down the highway as if I were on the Daytona speedway. My thoughts were spinning like the wheels on my car, driving my adrenaline to get me down to the hospital as quickly as I could. Finally, I had turned off the exit and was driving into the parking lot. I parked in the closest spot I could get to the entrance, got out, and walked down the same stone pathway through the automatic doors into the hospital. The people at the front desk stared at me as I approached to give them my name and my daughter's room number. Then, off to the elevator I went, anxious to see my little girl. I got off on the second floor and walked out onto the carpeting, which was designed with a path in mind. I walked through the hallway to Sophie's room passing the nurse's station along the way.

I arrived at the room and Peter began telling me about the events of the day. He was dreary, with defeat plastered across his face. As we were talking, the neurologist arrived. As I recall, he visited every evening. Once again he was getting Sophie off the bed to see if she could walk. He repeated the same neurological exam each day, waiting for her to walk as if by some miracle she would snap out it. I didn't understand his analysis of Sophie's predicament. It seemed logical to me that if she could not walk yesterday, there was a good probability that she wouldn't be able to walk today or tomorrow, but he continued to do the same exam. He looked over at us after he completed the exam that night and his facial expression gave no clue as to what was happening to my daughter. I just sat and watched complacently, trying to understand the relevance of this repetition.

That night I left the hospital to go home, as I needed to get to work the next day. Peter had called his mother, Lorraine, to see if she could come to the hospital. Of course she wanted to help, so she planned to drive up the next day to stay with Sophie. Peter and Lorraine would stay for the day and keep Sophie entertained. I would return to the hospital when I finished work in the evening. I felt like a small piece of pressure had been lifted from me.

The next day passed quickly with my mind on hiatus as to what was happening at the hospital. I was glad that I was busy so I didn't have to think about Sophie's next medical evaluation and what it would yield.

I felt a sense of relief all day. Then I arrived back in Sophie's room that evening. I was told by Lorraine that the psychologist had visited Sophie that day. Lorraine told me that she had a nice conversation with the psychologist. I sat down and listened to what Lorraine had to say. She went on talking about how nice the woman psychologist was to her and Sophie. Lorraine explained that she also added information about the family tree. They talked about Sophie at length regarding her personality, mood, attitude, and the present situation. Peter then told me that the psychologist had asked him questions about our family life. Lorraine had willingly joined the discussion with the psychologist. He reported to me that the psychologist had requested to meet with Sophie alone and he had complied. I listened attentively to what he was saying without any particular concern so far. It all seemed to be part of the routine evaluations that had been going on since we arrived at the hospital. Of course, I thought, the doctors needed to have a comprehensive assessment to come up with a diagnosis.

What I didn't realize, and couldn't have possibly imagined, was that there was a witch's brew in progress. A deceitful betrayal was about to impact the life of my family. What came next was so shocking that for a long moment it seemed that I could not even breathe. If I had never, ever known rage in my life, here was one of those rare moments when my cup runneth over. The rage inside of me burst forth in such a manner that my head hurt. I felt like a volcano about to erupt. I could feel my throat getting dry, preventing me from being able to swallow as Sophie's father spoke to me. "Well," he said, "the psychologist thinks that maybe Sophie is doing this because she misses you." He stared at me as he said the words slowly and carefully. "She [the psychologist] is thinking that Sophie really needs you," he said. "Sophie is upset that you work so much and she wants you to be home with her. The psychologist thinks that Sophie is doing this because she wants your attention." Lorraine piped in along with Peter, indicating that Sophie was exaggerating her symptoms. Now it was two against one and I was in the minority. If ever there was a time I felt alone it was now. I didn't know whether I wanted to crush my husband like I was Gulliver and he was a Lilliputian in Gulliver's Travels, or watch him fall into Dante's Inferno to pay up on his betrayal. I was so enraged. Whatever love we had shared turned to undeniable rage. Burning anger shot through me and I wanted to ram it right into his heart. How dare he take their side. It made it easier for him to agree with them now that he had the support of his mother in the conspiracy.

I was so angry I was nearly seeing double, but I slowed down my breathing and tried to get my words out calmly. "So you think what is happening to Sophie is all an act?" I could barely believe that I was saying this out loud, standing in the hall outside of the hospital room where Sophie lay alone. "Sophie does want your attention," he said. I could barely put any words together as adrenaline started running through my veins, but then suddenly, everything clicked.

"Are you kidding me or have you gone mad?" I said. "Do you really mean to tell me that you believe that this is all an act on her part?" Sophie's father looked at me with trepidation because he knew that he had crossed a line with me. Speaking in a near whisper, he said, "I think she may be doing this for attention."

Oh my God, I had just entered The Twilight Zone in my own life. I had never thought that would happen, that I would be in a world where I was the stranger from an alien planet. "No," I shouted. "I know my daughter and she would not stop walking because she wanted attention. There is no way I am buying that load of crap." I went on to defend her, saying, "Well, what about the pale, pasty look on her face, the excruciating pain that we sat and watched in the emergency room while we were waiting almost eight hours for her to be admitted? Why have they been giving her Motrin and Penicillin continuously if there is nothing wrong with her?"

Sophie's father looked at me and said, "It is hard to believe, but I think that maybe there is some truth to what they are saying." Of course she wanted my attention, I thought to myself. I was her mother for God's sake, and she wanted to be with me. What was wrong with Sophie wanting to be with her mother and telling someone else the way she felt? She was sick and wanted to be with her mother, me, because she was afraid. That made complete sense, but to turn this whole thing into a psychological disturbance was quite a stretch into fantasy.

How dare they make my daughter into a psychological conundrum? I wouldn't let that happen to her. There was no way I would allow these people who were called doctors but didn't know what was wrong with my daughter make her out to be a psychological experiment.

I knew I needed to take the anger that was brewing in me like a geyser about to explode and keep it for another time. I could not allow these angry feelings to take me away from my Sophie, who continued to lie idle in a hospital bed suffering with no answers. This concocted diagnostic picture could not deter me from my quest to find the truth that would help get my daughter well.

I was saddened by the fact that Sophie's father was buying into this dangerous fantasy to put an end to the unknown, but in a way, I understood it. It was hard to live life in limbo, not knowing what was wrong with our child. So it was understandable that he would rush to whatever answer he could hang on, so that he did not have to feel trapped by the unknown. I may have understood his position but was unable to accept that he had chosen the path of the psychologist and what she was proposing.

For me, the unknown was my path. It told me that I needed to push forward, to keep searching for the answer. The unknown was my energy force that guided me to new ideas, answers, and possibilities to help Sophie get well. Peter held the opposite view. He wanted it over right away. Any answer would do so that he did not have to consider searching for the answer. It was too hard for him to keep up pace with me, so he wanted to give in to the first answer that came along. I wouldn't let that happen to me—or to Sophie. There was no person that could pull me down into the underground. I wouldn't stop until I saw her smile, laugh, and run again. There had to be an answer out there in the universe, floating around, waiting for me to reach out and grab it. I would not be trapped into believing a made-up diagnosis to get my daughter out of the hospital. I couldn't pretend to know the intent of the hospital staff, but I would not give up the fight. Going forward was the only direction for me to take. I couldn't stop now.

Get your facts first,
then you can distort them
as you please.

—Mark Twain

There we were in the hospital day after day, watching the Motrin being provided without efficacy and the penicillin being provided for an infection that was unknown to all of us. Now, it was not only the doctors who bought into the idea that Sophie's not walking was basically all in her head—my own family had bought into it too. Who was to blame for all this chaos in my daughter's life? It was me, her mother—apparently the one person in her life who was just not giving her enough attention.

Could it be possible that a child could scream in pain for almost eight hours in an emergency room only to make it clear to her mother that she wanted her attention? It seemed apparent to everybody but me that a nine-year-old child could suddenly complain of various symptoms, including not being able to walk, just to get at her mother. Could it be feasible that a happy, outgoing child who had always been smiling could change overnight to an attention-seeking, manipulative, deviant child who was bordering on sociopathic tendencies as if she was taken over by the devil as in The Exorcist?

In the hospital I was beginning to feel like the medical professionals were presumptuously twisting information like con men because they were unable to get at the truth themselves. Their knowledge was limited and their tests were not giving any clues. The quickest way out of the dilemma for them was to conjure a psychological label. In my mind, this label represented their defeat, not mine. It was a cop-out, a way to take the pressure off themselves and to shift the reason for her problem to being a psychiatric episode. I felt as if I had just been the victim of a hit-and-run, left without witnesses or evidence. My head was spinning as if I had risen too quickly after sitting. I felt like I was losing my balance, and I desperately needed to gain a modicum of control over what was happening. The so-called "diagnosis" was traveling quickly, like a wildfire that I could not stop, and a strange chain of events was unfolding before me. Here in the hospital, the plan had taken off and I had no idea where it would end up. I watched and waited as the doctors began to spin their web—creating a story to explain everything.

That evening the neurologist came to see Sophie as usual. Sophie's father and I were sitting on either side of her on the bed. As soon as he entered the room, we jumped up and moved away from the bed to allow him access to our daughter—by now we were programmed to do this. He asked us how she was doing while he looked at her lying there. We said simultaneously, "She is the same," in exhausted, monotone voices. I stood and watched him do the same exam all over again for the gazillionth time. It was maddening to see him attempting to get Sophie to walk yet again. I felt as if I were being forced to watch the same horror video over and over again. When Sophie fell to the floor, he picked her up and placed her back on the bed in a sitting position.

The neurologist appeared to be surprised that Sophie was still unable to walk. It made me want to scream but I was gagged by my own thoughts, which, if I had made them known, would have had no impact upon this neurologist who was unable to see right in front of him. He smiled at us and requested to talk with us outside of Sophie's room. Together, Sophie's father and I followed the neurologist into the hallway. I turned to Sophie before exiting the room just to reassure her that we would just be outside of the room if she needed us. She continued to watch television as I said this to her, but she nodded.

The neurologist looked at us with compassion, as if he were confirming that we were caring parents even though we were ignorant of our daughter's machinations. As I recall, during the conversation he asked, "Is your daughter a bright girl?" He then went on to query us about how smart she actually was, as in whether she just had above-average intelligence or an actual high IQ. I was completely lost as to where this conversation was going. I didn't understand his direction or what he was getting at, but I continued to listen to him as his hypothetical prediction started to unfold. He began to tell us about a similar case involving a teenager who could not walk, but whose problem went away when he got the attention he was looking for from his parents.

Again, I was so shocked that the neurologist's words seemed to bounce off me, hitting the wall and coming right back to smack me in the face. I could not entertain such a preposterous supposition, nor could I believe that Sophie's father was buying this stuff. I felt alone inside, but I knew I had to act like I was part of the plan. I had to keep my poker face intact. The neurologist was being cautious as he spoke about this other case he had encountered. I realized that he was just another player on the stage of life, supporting the other medical professionals who, like actors, had laid the groundwork for this menacing diagnosis. All along, this neurologist had been one of the bad people, part of this evil plan of deception. It was obvious that the neurologist felt that it was imminent that some kind of diagnosis had to be made, whether it was real or imagined. Was this really happening to me? I could barely believe it. Why couldn't they say they just didn't know what was wrong with Sophie and send us somewhere else? Why did they have to save face by fabricating some kind of family dysfunction?

For the next few days, I went to work and returned to the hospital in the evening only to find out that yet another day had been uneventful with no answers. Peter stayed with Sophie until the early afternoon, then she was left in the hospital alone for a few ours until I arrived there late in the day. We would have dinner together and I would sleep through the night with her in the hospital, going to work the following morning after Peter had arrived. There was only one exception to the mundane daily events: The psychologist was coming daily to talk to Sophie. It was the psychologist that had been reporting to Peter some time in the morning after I was gone that she would be seeing Sophie every day. Now her illness had become a psychological forensic investigation—an intrusion into the mind of a nine-year-old child who desperately wanted to get better. Every day Sophie expressed her distress, worry, and fears to the psychologist.

She talked openly about her family and how much she needed us by her side, especially me. All of this information was transmitted innocently through friendly conversation. Little did Sophie realize that her inner fears were being interpreted as sick, attention-seeking behavior, and that she was seen as a creative child who was manipulatively trying to get her mother's attention by not walking.

After a few days of meeting with Sophie, the psychologist wanted to speak to this mother whom she had come to view as a cold, distant parent, continuing to work while her child was hospitalized, alienating her child further by intentionally not listening to her cries for help and attention. So off we went into the hallway for a conversation. Here stood the psychologist, telling me that she was basically forming an experimental hypothesis without fully understanding the damaging and debilitating effects it could have on Sophie and the rest of us. And here I stood, finding it hard to believe that I was facing reality, that it wasn't all a bad dream. I couldn't comprehend how these doctors could possibly be real people who thought that my daughter's physical pain was just a matter of psychological distress. As I recall, the conversation went as follows:

"Hi," she said.

I nodded back at her.

"How are you doing today?"

"Okay," I answered. Can we get to the point of this conversation?"Well your daughter is quite upset."

"I agree, I know she is quite upset."

"Sophie's concerned about you working and not having enough time to spend with her."

"Yes, I understand that she is upset about that."

"What do you think you can do to help her?"

"I suppose I would need to think about that."

"Could you work part-time?"

"Right now I am concerned about my daughter's physical illness and what you and the hospital staff are doing about that."

"So you think she has a medical condition?"

"I think so as she has been in physical pain since we arrived at the hospital several days ago. The medical staff has been giving her penicillin and Motrin since the doctor saw her upon her arrival to her room here. So the idea of a medical condition is quite plausible to me. Don't you think?"

"Well aren't tests being completed?"

"Yes, there are tests."

"She still is quite upset about you not being available for her."

Blah, Blah, Blah.

"I know that she is upset, she is physically sick and that would upset anyone."

"I can see that you may be finding it hard to accommodate your daughter's needs."

Help me lord find the patience to soothe my anger.

"I'm not sure what you are trying to say."

"Only that your daughter needs you."

"I think I get that and I need to be with her right now."

I turned and walked back into Sophie's room to be with her. I went over to her and sat down on the bed, hugged her, kissed her cheek, and told her I loved her.

Then I went to the pull-out sofa to make my bed ready for sleep.

I felt like disaster was reaching over to grab me and throw me down, but I refused to buy into the psychologist's theory. As for Peter, the desperation for an answer to his daughter's problems had taken over his better judgment. I knew that my daughter was suffering real pain, and I was going to find the answers. No matter what it took, I would find someone who was willing to listen to Sophie. That was the one thing that I could be sure of making happen.

The best way out is always through.

—Robert Frost

The Hospital Stay–The Last Two Days

As I researched Lyme disease, I found that there was not a great deal of information about it. I found articles that raised questions about the Lyme test itself. Why were people who did not have a positive Lyme test still getting sick? I also discovered something called Lyme Syndrome, which referred to people who continued to have symptoms even after they were treated for the recommended twenty-one days. The hospital had never ruled out Lyme disease, but none of the doctors had ever really considered it a possibility either.

The more I read about Lyme disease, the more I realized the depth of its mystery. There were more questions about Lyme disease than there were answers. In fact, I myself would never have considered Lyme disease if my daughter had not had two tick bites and I hadn't seen the ticks and removed them myself. But why were the doctors at the hospital dismissing Lyme disease as a possible diagnosis? I could not get a straight answer. I had to find out for myself, so each night after visiting Sophie I delved into researching Lyme disease and, eventually, other tick-borne illnesses that also wreaked havoc in people's lives.

By now it was more than evident that there were no answers at the hospital for Sophie. The next day I went back knowing that the talk about discharging Sophie was coming very soon. The doctor overseeing my daughter's case was barely visible. It was the psychologist who informed us that they were getting close to discharging Sophie. I questioned as to where she would be discharged in her condition and the doctors started talking about physical therapy and psychiatry. Her symptoms did not warrant care in a rehabilitation center so she was coming home with us. The treatment plan meeting for Sophie's discharge would be the following day.

The next morning, Sophie's father and I waited in her hospital room for the treatment plan meeting to begin. Sophie had been taken to an activity in the children's ward so that she would not hear what was being said about her illness and care. The only two professionals participating in the conference were the doctor and the psychologist. There was no explanation as to why only they were here for the conference and not the neurologist. The psychologist began the meeting by mentioning how much she had enjoyed talking with Sophie and what a wonderful child she was. Well, of course, I already knew my Sophie was special. I stayed quiet, placing a mental lock on my tongue. The psychologist continued describing the talks she had been having with Sophie. Calmly, I observed and listened, hanging onto each word, waiting for the final dagger to be thrown my way. Finally, the psychologist came out with how Sophie needed her mother and that I needed to reduce my workload and start working part-time to be available for her. She said Sophie's behavior was a cry for help. It was never said that her not walking was specifically a cry for help, just that her behavior in general was a cry for help. But what behavior were we talking about exactly?

I was sitting on the vinyl sofa, further away from the two of them than Peter, who sat on the hospital bed. The psychologist was looking at me most of the time while she was talking, so I knew that I was seen as the culprit. I was the worst mother of all mothers, who forgot to spend time with my daughter and did not consider her feelings about what she needed from me.

I could not believe what I was hearing—yes, my ears were burning and the flames were about to explode into the atmosphere. I sat there and watched as the words flowed effortlessly off their tongues. While their voices passed right through me, Peter's eyes began to tear. I watched him trying to hold back the flow of tears, which left him gasping and choking for air. I knew that he was thinking that what they were saying was true. For a moment, my own eyes watered from seeing him in pain, exposed, but all I had left was my composure and I would not let them crush me.

The psychologist looked at me for a response. I turned my head in her direction and said, "So what is it you are recommending?" I knew they were expecting a hysterical, what-the-hell-are-you-talking-about response to the attack on my motherhood, but I also knew that it would be meaningless to lash out and reject their proposition. They had made up their minds. The hospital needed a diagnosis, so this was it, in a nutshell. The professionals appeared delighted that I asked what was being recommended. The psychologist went on to say that Sophie would need a psychiatrist, a therapist, and physical therapy. The psychologist relayed the message that she was quite interested in working with Sophie herself. They had already engaged in a therapeutic relationship and it would make it easier for Sophie to continue to work with her. The psychologist felt quite confident that Sophie would get better with psychotherapy and physical therapy.

The doctor sat there quietly and nodded in agreement with the psychologist. Peter continued crying. I could barely keep myself intact watching him. Then it happened—I lost the control I had so desperately tried to keep and tears rolled down my cheeks. My emotions overwhelmed me. Silence filled the room until I was able to get my wits back by asking who was going to arrange the services. It was explained that a social worker would make the arrangements for physical therapy. I made sure the psychologist understood that we would be finding a therapist closer to home. Peter expressed concern about finding a psychiatrist as the priority. In annoyance, I told him he could locate one himself.

I was filled with anger as I tried to absorb what had just happened. It was a miscarriage of justice. I wanted to find a medical doctor who knew anything at all about Lyme disease. Then I realized that the woman in the local restaurant had given me a doctor's name. I must contact him. The only way I was going to agree to Sophie being discharged the following morning was if I left the hospital with all of her medical records. I requested a copy of her entire medical record and was assured that I would get everything I needed.

The next morning I arrived at the hospital at about seven a.m. I sat outside of Sophie's room until I was able to speak with the nurse. Finally, the nurse stopped her paperwork, looked up at me, and asked, "Can I help you?" I told her that Sophie was being discharged and I needed a copy of her medical records. First she told me that she couldn't get a copy of Sophie's medical records. Then she said the medical records were outsourced and I would have to write a request for her records. She transmitted all of this information in a matter-of-fact manner with no emotion or reaction to my request. My blood started to boil, but I listened attentively. Then I said, in a volume that would shake Mt. Kilimanjaro, "I am taking my daughter out of this hospital in a wheelchair, with a walker, with no answers about what is happening to her, and you are telling me I have to write a request for her records!" I was completely exasperated and I didn't care what she thought of me. I went on to say, "I am not leaving this hospital—and my daughter will not be discharged—until I get every piece of paperwork that exists in her record." The nurse looked up at me with agitation and replied, "I will contact the nurse manager." I looked her in the eye and said in a forceful tone, "I think that would be a good idea." Then I walked away and sat down to wait.

After about thirty minutes, a nurse manager walked over to the station nurse, who pointed to me. I repeated that I would not be leaving the hospital with my daughter in a wheelchair and no answers as to what was wrong with her without a copy of her records. The manager got me in contact with someone in the record department whom I spoke to on the phone from the nurses' station. He told me the same thing about requiring a written request for the records. Outraged, I had no other choice but to let this man have a piece of my uncensored mind. After venting my rage, I told him that I would not leave the hospital until I got a copy of my daughter's records, and that I was sure ABC, NBC, and CBS TV stations would be interested in my story. He got irate and told me not to threaten him or I wouldn't get anything. After that, we engaged in a somewhat rational conversation about the situation regarding my daughter and he told me exactly where I could go in the hospital to get a copy of her records.

Well, that old saying about the squeaky wheel is, in fact, the truth. I never thought I would have to rant and rave and make threats to get Sophie's records. However, it didn't matter what I needed to do to get those records—I would have jumped through hoops of fire. Finally I had the records in my hands. I could leave the hospital with my daughter and begin searching for a doctor who would actually help her.

There is nothing like staying at home for real comfort.

—Jane Austen

After getting Sophie's medical records, I woke her up to tell her we were leaving the hospital. She was drained and worn to the bone but happy to be going home. As happy as she could be knowing that she was still sick and the doctors had no answers for her. She told me she was afraid when we arrived home and explained that she believed I was the only person who knew how she really felt. Sophie believed in me, her mother. I had to believe that she would get better. It was an awakening to realize that solving this mystery was going to be a long road but I was determined to get her well. Giving up was not an option.

Slowly, Sophie got up and asked me for help to get to the bathroom. She was unable to manage walking so I carried her to the bathroom and positioned her on the toilet seat. Afterwards, I helped her wash her hands and face and brush her teeth. Then we returned to the bed where she sat as I packed up her stuff. I got her dressed and into the wheelchair. As we left the room, I stared for a moment at the carpeted path to the elevator, silently saying my farewell. Then I pushed Sophie in the wheelchair down the carpeted hallway to the elevator. At last we were outside of the hospital. The nightmare hospital stay had come to an end.

It was a crisp March day. I felt the cold hit me and a chill swiftly pass through my body. Slowly, I pushed the wheelchair to the car. I was determined to make a fresh start. I got Sophie into the car, secured her seatbelt, closed the wheelchair, opened the hatchback, and placed the wheelchair into the back of the car. I laid the walker on top of the wheelchair with a noisy clang and closed the hatchback. I got into the car and sat down with a sigh, ready to go home. Quickly, I looked in the rearview mirror to get a glimpse of Sophie in the backseat. Sophie's eyes conveyed the depth of her fear, and I knew that she was experiencing the kind of fright that paralyzes the body. She was enduring an agony that she was unable to understand. There was the unspoken question. Would she ever be able to walk again?

As I drove home Sophie and I chatted about getting her into the house with the wheelchair. I was trying to explain how she was going to get up the stairs and maneuver herself around. She listened and responded with a "Yes Mom I get it." For most of the ride, she just stared out the car window. I'd look at the road and then back to Sophie, waiting for her to let her feelings go. I did not know when or how she would be able to process the unimaginable distress she was experiencing. I thought that trying to get her to talk about what was happening to her would make her feel better. In reality, it just made it all the more real and absolutely frightening for her. So I let the quiet be her peace of mind even if it was for only a brief time. I left her alone because I did not want her to feel like I was badgering her to talk about the most difficult challenge of her life. When and if she was ever ready to say something I would be waiting to hear it.

Finally we were home. I got the wheelchair out of the car and around to her door, and told her to take her time getting out. She looked up at me helplessly, like a fallen leaf ready to hit the ground. She was unable to move her legs, so I shifted her to position her in the wheelchair, moving her as if I were handling a mannequin, and pushed the wheelchair to the front door. Once inside the house, I instructed Sophie to use her arms to lift her body up each step to her room on the second floor. At first it was awkward, but she managed it successfully. Then I closed the wheelchair, carried it up the stairs, and reopened it so she could be mobile around the house. The wheelchair glided easily between her bedroom and the bathroom. She now had to learn to manage living from a wheelchair. This reality had cut through me like a knife. The life of our family had once been a place of comfort but that had been swept away by a tsunami of change. We were now all angry people trying to deal with life's mishaps, ready at any time to explode at each other. Our anger was a dark cloud hanging over us, ready to turn into a tornado without warning. I had to be with Sophie every waking moment that I was able when I wasn't working, but it would be at the expense of the rest of the family. This was my mission, and I was going to follow it like a monk on the path of a holy one.

No sooner had we settled in when the phone rang. It was my sister-in-law, Lisa, calling to tell me she had purchased a DVD of Under Our Skin, a documentary on Lyme disease, for us. I appreciated her taking the time to do this. She told me that she had watched the DVD already and wanted to prepare me for what I would be seeing. As I listened, my chest tightened. I was quiet as she told me that what was in the documentary was unpleasant and worrisome. I felt sick to my stomach while listening to her—so much so that it would take me nearly three weeks to bring myself to watch it. After it arrived in the mail, I put it next to the television and kept picking it up and staring at the cover day after day until I was able to get up the courage to watch it. When I did, I made sure I was alone in the house because I didn't want anyone else to see it and panic.

The documentary presents the cruel reality of Lyme disease, which made me feel like a gun was being pushed into the back of my neck. Who would have thought that we were a society trying to restrict and, in some cases, revoke the licenses of doctors who were willing to help those suffering the ravages of Lyme disease? I was left baffled by the fact that heartless politicking was going on while patients were helplessly having their internal organs savagely invaded by Lyme disease and had no say as to their care.

However, this was not the case with Dr. Daniel Cameron (who was identified by the lyme community as a Lyme Literate Medical Doctor,which is currently not a medically accepted term), who I would be contacting to set up an appointment for Sophie. The next day, I called Dr. Cameron's office and told one of his staff members Sophie's story. The woman listened attentively to me and did not cut me off, put me on hold, or stop me as I recounted the long nightmare of events. With some surprise, I realized that she was not surprised at all with what I was telling her.

Once I had completed the story, she asked if I wanted to make an appointment. I said yes, but that I wasn't sure what day I could make it. I told her I would call her back. Why I did not make an appointment that day or take Sophie to the office immediately is beyond my comprehension. I can only surmise that I was still in shock due to the stress of what had happened at the hospital, and therefore wasn't sure what to do next.

In the days that followed, Sophie adjusted to being back home in the wheelchair. We tried to make life as normal as possible. I knew that Sophie was not herself— she looked pale, pasty, and sad. She was also quite angry as she felt isolated and alienated from the world she had known. I wasn't sure whether I would ever see any joy in Sophie's face again, but I could not say that out loud— and somehow I could not make myself believe it. I hoped that she would get better, but it wasn't enough to hope—I had to know that she would get better. I had to be the one person that would not let her down.

How long it would take and what I would have to live through to get Sophie better remained unknown. All I knew was that we had to journey into the darker side of Lyme disease. I believed that darkness would be upon us before we saw any light.

If way to the better there be,
it exacts a full look at the worst.

—Thomas Hardy

Sophie's first weekend home from the hospital started off calmly—until Saturday evening. By then she had been home for just four days and was becoming restless. In fact, she was becoming visibly agitated. I could tell that she was not feeling like herself. The expression on her face told me something was changing inside her, but I could not put my finger on it. At that point I wasn't thinking about how the hospital stay may have impacted her. I knew she was angry, but I just didn't know how angry or how much Lyme disease would play a part in the emotional instability that was about to unfold. Looking back, I never could have imagined that the Borrelia Burgdorferi bacteria, that which causes Lyme disease, could wreak such havoc on a child's mind.

When Peter and I heard noises coming from her room we walked down the hallway to see what was going on. Sophie was throwing things, thrashing her arms about, and screaming at the top of her lungs. I asked her what was going on, but she did not stop. She kept spinning her wheelchair around as she thrashed about, not even noticing us standing there. I tried to grab her to make her look me in the eye, but it was useless. I saw a stranger inside my daughter looking back at me. Her eyes were empty, but I kept talking to her, trying to get a response. Peter just stood there and watched as she kept moving about wildly, screaming sounds without forming words. No intervention would get her to stop and calm down. She was exhibiting behavior that we had never seen in any of our children.

Peter and I stood together in her room trying to decide what to do to next. We felt so lost in our own home with our own daughter. We tried to comfort her, but it was of no use, we needed help. So after a brief back-and-forth outside of her room, we decided that she needed to go to the hospital, but we decided to take her to another hospital. Secretly, I was hoping that another hospital would know more.

We had to get Sophie into the car, but first we had to get her calmed down as best we could so she would cooperate. Once inside the car, Peter sat with her in the back seat for her safety and protection. I drove to the hospital. Sophie screamed for the entire ride. I watched her and Peter in the rearview mirror as much as I could, as she was still very agitated. Her father was gentle though, and held her close to him so she would not hurt herself. No words would provide any comfort for her, but we kept trying to say things that would calm her. Sophie continued to thrash about. Her screaming did not subside in the least bit throughout the entire ride. Peter did all he could do to keep her safe in his arms.

Finally we arrived at the hospital emergency room with Sophie in the wheelchair. Still she was unable to stop screaming. The staff began to notice that there was a child who wouldn't stop screaming, and the noise was becoming disruptive to the emergency room environment so a staff person came and directed us to a separate room. Together, Peter and I held her hands as she lay on the gurney half crazed and exhausted from screaming. My middle daughter Molly and her closest friend Elisa had accompanied us to the hospital to help, and although they stayed through it all, they were frightened by what they were seeing. The two of them stood there gaping at Sophie, trying to understand what was happening to the little girl that often tortured them to be part of their teenage conversation. "Help me mommy, please help me," Sophie screamed as if begging for her life at the guillotine. She was squeezing my hand so hard it was cutting off my circulation. Then, "AAAAAAAAAAAAAA!!!!!!!!!!!!" she screamed. There was the tiniest moment of silence as she grabbed another breath of fresh air. On and on went her bone-chilling and ear-piercing screams. "Mommy, Daddy, help me, please, please, help me!" But then in between screams she began to beg us softly, as if she were barely getting enough air, "Please, get it out of me, please, I feel it crawling inside of me," and then another screech would follow. Her eyes were piercing as she pleaded, "Help me, mommy, get it out of me, get it out of me," taking short staccato breaths.

Finally the doctor arrived. He asked me to go out into the hallway, where he told me he was thinking of giving her Haldol and Ativan to calm her down, treating me like a colleague. Thank goodness, I knew something about psychotropic medications. I said I wanted to try the Ativan first to see if that did the job. I wanted to avoid Haldol if possible, because it would put my daughter into an almost vegetative state. The doctor agreed, and we discussed how the medication was to be given. I requested the injection because it would be a quicker means of absorption.

After the speedy dialogue in the hallway, the doctor told the nurse to give Sophie the injection of Ativan. Peter and I held her steady, reassuring her as the nurse took out the needle to inject her thigh. She screamed right through the injection. Minutes passed as we waited to see if her eyelids would start getting heavy. After about fifteen minutes her eyes began closing, her breathing became slower, and her screams grew softer. Then her eyelids closed and she was asleep.

As we sat waiting for the discharge papers, Peter asked the doctor what he thought of our daughter's episode. I recall the conversation that took place in this way: "What would you do if this was your kid?" Peter asked. The doctor looked him straight in the eye and said, "I would get her a good psychiatrist." I knew for sure that the doctors at this hospital were not informed about the symptoms of Lyme disease. They did not have a clue about what was going on. Peter thanked the doctor as he grabbed the prescription for the Ativan and off we went. Together, we carried Sophie into the car. Once inside, Peter couldn't help but tell me how important it was to find a psychiatrist. "I know, I know," I said. I was too tired to fight, so I agreed, just to keep the peace.

The truth is lived not taught.

—Hermann Hesse

I Am Not Alone

The next morning, Sunday, I was relieved to see that the Ativan seemed to be working. I decided to run out for a cup of coffee by myself. I needed time to listen to my own breathing and nurture what little sense of sanity I had left. I sat in the car drinking a large Dunkin' Donuts coffee and dialed Dr. Cameron's office. A man answered. I told him who I was, and he told me that he was Dr. Cameron. I was amazed to be speaking to a doctor in his office on a Sunday morning. Stunned, I fumbled at forming sounds into words and words into sentences to get out Sophie's story. Dr. Cameron listened quietly. When I told him that I would like to bring Sophie to see him he scheduled her for the following day. I felt a sense of relief floating over me. I knew that this was Sophie's chance.

When I returned home Peter seemed upset. "Where were you?" he asked in a frightened tone. "I just went out to get a cup of coffee," I responded. "Sophie needs you," he told me. I nodded and went to her room. I sat by her, brushing my hand down the side of her face to give her some comfort. She tried to absorb the tenderness, but the pain of what had occurred and the fear of what was to come were written on her face.

The doorbell rang and I went downstairs to open the door for a woman who introduced herself as the nurse who had been sent by the hospital to assess Sophie for physical therapy. I welcomed her and brought her up to Sophie's room. We all sat down and the nurse asked Sophie what had happened to her. Sophie was too tired to go through the litany of events. Suddenly I realized that the fatigue that plagued her is a common symptom of Lyme disease. She was practically paralyzed with exhaustion. I started to tell the story while Sophie sat quietly, filling in the story here and there. The nurse asked to speak with Sophie alone, and after Sophie nodded at me to let me know that it was okay with her, I left her there alone with the nurse and went downstairs to the living room to wait.

About fifteen minutes later, the nurse came downstairs to complete the insurance paperwork and advise me of the physical therapy schedule. While the nurse was getting ready to leave, Sophie called me upstairs and when I got there I could see she was in distress. Just after I heard the front door close behind the nurse, Sophie started to scream with rage, smashing her pillow and thrashing it back and forth as hard as she could. I tried to talk to her but she was lost in fear and explosive terror. I had no words to make her feel safe, so I tried to hold her. After a while she submitted to my hugging her. I felt useless as I hugged her close and told her I loved her. "Why, Mommy, why is this happening to me?" she cried. "I don't know why this happened to you," I told her, "but I will not stop looking for answers to get you well. If it is the only thing I am able to do, then that is what I will do." She stopped struggling and listened to me, even while she continued to cry, so I knew that she had heard me in the midst of her catharsis.

That night the nurse called me again. The first thing she said to me, as I recall the conversation, was, "Your daughter's problem is not psychological." That statement was the first sign of real hope coming from a nurse. "Why is it that you think it is not psychological?" I asked. The nurse told me that her sister had a friend in Ohio whose daughter had suffered something similar to what Sophie was going through. The nurse offered me the phone number of the woman in Ohio and recommended that I call her. She believed that this person could give me information on where to get help for Sophie.

I was stunned by what had just occurred, yet I felt validated by this confirmation of my own belief that Sophie's illness was medical, not psychiatric, in origin. Had a miracle knocked at my door that day the nurse arrived? Somehow I knew that this particular nurse had been meant to come to my home. I took down the phone number, feeling like a hungry dog, wondering whether I should call the woman in Ohio or wait until the next day. No, I decided, I would call her right away. She might give me another clue to help me solve the long list of riddles leading to answers.

I picked up the phone again and dialed. When the woman answered, I briefly told her how I got her number and why I was calling and added that I was extremely anxious to hear what she had to say. The story the woman shared with me about her daughter was horrifying but it was also calming to know that someone else out there in the universe was going through a similar circumstance. She told me that her daughter's Lyme disease had gone undiagnosed for many years. Her words were like jewels found at the end of a treasure hunt. I hung on to every syllable as she told me that I must find a Lyme Literate Medical Doctor (LLMD). I couldn't believe there was such a thing as a doctor who specifically worked with patients with Lyme disease, but I knew that a whole new world of information had opened for me.

There was almost too much to absorb. She told me about a doctor in Connecticut, a pediatric neurologist who treats children with Lyme disease, and that she traveled regularly from Ohio to Connecticut to have him treat her daughter. This doctor had given her daughter immunoglobulin injections for the past several months, which was really helping to boost her daughter's immune system as well as decrease her debilitating fatigue. She recommended that I see Dr. Charles Ray Jones in Connecticut, and informed me that he treated many children suffering with Lyme disease. He was considered to be the go-to doctor for children with Lyme disease, she reported. All of this was foreign to me, but I listened. It never registered with me until later, when I read Stephen Buhner's book, Healing Lyme Naturally, that supporting the immune system was critical to wellness. This information significantly changed how I helped my daughter.

The woman went on to tell me about all of the doctors she had taken her daughter to see and how they had told her that she was too close to her daughter and had caused her emotional problems that led to her illness. No longer enraged, I was astonished by the fact that we had both received a psychiatric diagnosis as an explanation for our daughters' Lyme symptoms. This was the second significant piece of information that helped me move along in my search to help Sophie. I now knew for certain that Lyme disease was the culprit. The realization of this knowledge confirmed that this was going to be a long voyage to wellness for my daughter. I went to sleep that night no longer feeling like I was in the dark, no longer feeling like I was alone. It was as if a glowing light had filled my mind. I believed it was the light of hope that would now be my constant companion.

But what we call our despair
is often only the painful
eagerness of unfed hope.

—George Eliot

The Doctor Visit

The next day I woke up Sophie and helped her get dressed. We were going to see Dr. Daniel Cameron, who I had discovered the night before was also a Lyme Literate Medical Doctor. On Dr. Cameron's website I found out about the International Lyme and Associated Disease Society (ILADS), which represents a group of doctors who hold a different viewpoint about Lyme disease and its treatment. The ILADS group educates doctors on Lyme disease based on their experiences treating patients with Lyme and research facilitated by these physicians. These doctors are the medical professionals making efforts to treat their patients diagnosed with Lyme disease by reviewing their symptoms. The diagnosis is made by a collection of data beyond the unreliable Elisa/Western Blot test that may or may not have the required number of IgG and IgM bands to be interpreted as a positive result for Lyme disease.

Sophie and I left early for the doctor's office, as we were the first appointment of the day. While waiting in the lounge area, Sophie sat slumped in her wheelchair, looking around the room. She began talking loudly, becoming more and more agitated about how no one was going to be able to help her. At that moment, I noticed the office staff staring at us. I got Sophie to quiet down for a couple of minutes until she noticed a framed magazine cover on the wall. The magazine cover story was about the top doctors in New York State's Westchester County, and Dr. Cameron was included. Sophie peered at it with disbelief and then started pointing at it and screamed at me, "Huh? This doctor is the best? No, he's the worst!" Just then we heard Sophie's name called and a woman in a white medical coat beckoned to us. I got up and pushed Sophie's wheelchair down a long hallway to the exam room. Sophie sat quietly in her wheelchair, looking defeated. When Dr. Cameron entered, she turned to face the wall. "Hello," Dr. Cameron said. He sat down at the desk and tried to communicate with Sophie, but she was angry, discouraged, and fearful. He told me that he had reviewed all the hospital lab test results and paperwork. "It was good," he said, "that the hospital took all these tests, as it helps to rule out other possibilities." Sophie grew increasingly agitated as the doctor talked to me about her condition, which he concluded, as I recall, was neurologic Lyme disease.

As I tried to explain where we were at now, Sophie started moving her wheelchair, banging into the wall of the newly-painted office. I tried to communicate with her but it was of no use. She kept pushing the metal edge of the wheelchair foothold into the wall, creating a dent. I told Dr. Cameron about the recent hospital event and that Sophie had been prescribed Ativan to calm her down. Sophie had her back turned to us and started yelling at the wall, "I will never be able to walk again. This is how it will be for me. No one can help me, not even you. I don't know why we are even here!" As her agitation increased, I feared that she might erupt in an explosion right there in the office that I would not be able to contain. I looked at the doctor and suggested that I give her an Ativan, and he agreed. "You have to take this," I told her firmly, and she complied willingly.

I knew that the medication would not take effect immediately, so I sat there, waiting for the Ativan to work and watching for any further unpredictable changes. In the midst of this episode, the doctor went on to review Sophie's symptoms and the various groups of antibiotics available. I was well aware from my research that doxycycline was the medication of choice, especially since, according to Dr. Cameron, Sophie had had a negative reaction to amoxicillin.

I felt a rush of relief: Finally we had a medication that could probably help her. But first I had to get Sophie back home and pick up the prescription from the pharmacy. We left the office in a bedraggled mess of emotional weariness.

About fifteen to twenty minutes into the drive home, Sophie began screaming and thrashing around in the back seat. I tried to calm her down without any success, and realized that I needed to stop the car, so I began racing to the next rest area. She was exploding in the back seat, kicking the window so hard I feared it would break. Finally I was able to pull over. I got into the back seat and held her to prevent her from harming herself. I was talking to her, and although it appeared that she wasn't listening, I knew she was there with me and heard my voice. But she was unable to control herself and I felt as if I were holding an exploding bomb in my hands.

Lost as to what to do next, I got another Ativan to give her. Sophie continued to thrash around as I struggled to position her to take the pill. "It will be okay," I told her over and over again. "I am here. I love you." I repeated the words over and over like a mantra until she had exhausted herself and collapsed limply onto the seat. I got her seatbelt back on her and hopped back into the driver's seat, hoping I would be able to get home as fast as I could without further incident.

Finally, I pulled into our driveway with a sigh of relief. Sophie was visibly tired from the Ativan. I got her into the house and into bed and called her father to tell him to pick up the doxycycline at the pharmacy. He agreed. I went on to tell him the story of the doctor visit and the ride home. He told me how difficult it is for him to concentrate on work with all this happening. "We must get a psychiatrist going," he said. "Okay," I told him, irritably, "I will do it."

Up until now, the days had passed with Sophie looking more and more exhausted. Her energy level had been dissipating rather than increasing. She was still unable to go to school so she was receiving home tutoring. All she could manage to do was an hour of schoolwork with the tutor. After the tutoring session, she would collapse. Sophie spent most of the time in bed, daydreaming and staring at the television, trying to either make sense of or be distracted from her new reality. The only time she would perk up a bit was whenever I joined her for a little while to watch the Food Network. We would talk about what we would like to make and act as food critics, commenting on the foods being prepared. She told me our food banter took her mind off everything else.

What had happened to my little girl? As I waited for Sophie's father to bring home the prescription of doxycycline, a painful realization hit me in the gut. I wanted to cry and scream out to someone about this feeling of injustice, but not a single syllable ever emerged from my mouth. This was now my life and I felt like I had been hit by a knockout punch in the first round. But I knew that I needed to harness my anger and turn it into energy to keep up the search for answers. It was my quest to help her get better. I needed to believe in Sophie and myself, to have the faith that an answer was out there for me to find. Sophie's life had become a frenzy of unanticipated events. Her happiness had become a distant memory. And because of that, our family was struggling with this new state of discomfort called despair. We couldn't talk to one another without the agony of Sophie's predicament leaking into the dialogue. Any conversation could erupt into a frustrating exchange because I was always with Sophie in her room when I wasn't working. I was always making food for Sophie, lying in the bed with Sophie watching television, falling asleep with Sophie. I did not cook much for the family, or spend much time with anyone else but Sophie. I was not there for them in the way they would have liked me to be, the way that I had been all the years before Sophie got sick. They felt abandoned. Even though they understood what was necessary for me to do, it was a bitter pill for them to swallow. Watching Sophie fall into the physically immobilizing fatigue of Lyme disease every day kept us all on edge. I knew that Peter's greatest fear was that Sophie would not come out of it and he would have to take care of her in her present state for the rest of our lives. One day he told me that he did not think he was capable of taking care of her like she was if she never got better. My answer was simple. "She will get better, I know it." I suppose he did not understand where I got my strength from and how I was able to do it day after day. For me it was never a question or a choice to be made. Taking care of my daughter and searching for answers was a matter of survival. I believe that survival is something we do. It is a behavior not a thought process.

The only source of knowledge is experience.

—Albert Einstein

The next day Sophie began the doxycycline regimen, 250 mg. twice a day. I had been feeling imprisoned by the unknown and now, for the first time, it was as if I had been given the hope of a key to my release. I knew inside that this medication was going to change things and I hoped it would bring my little girl back to me. I felt confident that she would walk again. But Sophie's father didn't share my confidence. He was skeptical, nervous, and unsure. His pessimism absorbed his better judgment and any rational thought. He felt that our life as a family as we had always known it was over. It was a dismal discovery. Shattered, he sank into sadness. He thought that our daughter had been lost, had a mental breakdown of some sort. But I knew differently, and I kept on believing that she would walk again, and the image of her walking that I carried with me was slowly turning into a reality.

Sophie was getting physical therapy at home to help strengthen her legs. She was becoming proficient at maneuvering around the house in the wheelchair. Her appetite was good and she was able to sleep through the night, at least most nights. She still often experienced horrific nightmares—night terrors during which she would scream at the sight of people being killed in her mind as if she were locked in a horror film with no way out. When she awakened from one of these dreams, she was at first unable to separate the nightmare from reality. She struggled to find a way back to reality. Her screaming was unbearable, yet I could not allow myself to separate from her as she held on to me. Something was out there after her, she would tell me as she hid her face in my arm. I always tried to reassure her that nothing was out there, but she would scream anyway with a rasp that was almost primitive. "It's out there mommy and it is coming after me and you and Daddy," she panted. "Someone will get hurt and I won't be able to stop it!"

To Sophie, doom was lurking around every corner and in every crack and crevice of her room, holding her hostage, threatening her sanity. I was unable to calm her down so I would just hold her close, saying over and over again, "Everything will be okay, you will be okay, I won't let anything hurt you, I love you." I'd repeat this mantra until she fell asleep from sheer exhaustion. As sleep overcame her, there was always a feeling of peacefulness and a sense of relief. But I too felt tortured by her nightmares. Knowing that I was unable to stop those scary dreams I became completely consumed by her dread of what was to come. Together we traveled this road of despair, waiting, hoping to find a way out.

But miraculously, after a few weeks on doxycycline, Sophie was actually feeling slightly better. It was just a smidgen of progress, but it was hopeful. Home schooling continued for one hour a day, three days a week. Sophie was still unable to cope with more than that due to extreme fatigue. Two weeks later, we returned to Dr. Cameron for a follow-up visit. This visit was not volatile like the first one, but even though she was less agitated, she was still sad, pale, and angry. But even that could be considered a step in a positive direction, so I was grabbing hold of it.

Once in the exam room, Dr. Cameron tried to communicate with Sophie, but again she turned to look at the wall. She was still in a wheelchair and did not believe he could help her. But regardless of her attempts to distance herself from him, the doctor continued to reach out and communicate with her. He wanted to know what was happening to her from her perspective. "Why should I talk to you? What can you do for me? No one has been able to help me, look at me," she said with a sob. "I feel like I will be this way for the rest of my life." Hearing her say those words was like someone ripping my heart out with their bare hands.

Even then, Dr. Cameron still tried to engage her in a dialogue. Most of the doctors I had known would have run for the hills by now. He even tried to cajole her, but she was too angry to respond. I recounted the events of the past two weeks and told him we just needed to keep going. After we left the office, Sophie told me that she was hungry, so we went to get something to eat. I was relieved that her appetite was strong, but time outside had to be limited as her behavior was still unpredictable. I could no longer anticipate her every move. So we were continuing with the Ativan, even though I believed that this was just a temporary solution to the problem of her rage outbursts.

Dr. Cameron had suggested that Sophie return to school so that her life could be as normal as possible. This way, she would not be isolated and could interact with her friends. So I decided to move in that direction. After a couple of weeks of being homeschooled, arrangements were made for a special bus to take Sophie to school in her wheelchair. We started out with a half-day of school. Although she still tired easily, this was a step forward.

Sophie showed some enthusiasm about returning to school, but she also wore a look of dismay. She was concerned about her ability to cope and seemed to have lost the confidence that had been building inside her. Her fragile assuredness had been severed by this illness. Nevertheless, she complied with the doctor's and her mother's recommendation that returning to school, even for a half-day could help her feel like she once again had the normal routine of a child her age.

At first, the wheelchair gave Sophie a special status. The kids in her class appeared to be happy to see her and she believed in their sincere interest in her medical dilemma. However, they constantly asked her what happened, like woodpeckers marking their favorite tree. She told them that she had Lyme disease, but they acted as if she was speaking in a foreign language, and she felt like a new student from some godforsaken land. Sophie was confounded as to what it was she could possibly tell them when she could barely understand what was happening to her.

"Mom, the kids at school keep asking me what's wrong when I put my head down on my desk," she told me. "Why do they keep asking me? I tell them that I have Lyme disease, but they keep asking what is wrong with me." I listened attentively to her and tried to conjure up some possible answers for her to offer in order to hold off the constant questioning, but I knew that it was utterly useless. Those children were afraid of her, and that was a problem I couldn't fix. Sophie did not want to hurt their feelings. The disease had not corrupted her kindness toward the human condition. She desperately wanted to explain what was happening to her.

The teacher and I made an agreement that when Sophie felt tired or frustrated that she could lay her head down on the table and rest. It worked some of the time when her peers left her alone, but often they could not. Their curiosity and concern made them approach her to see if she was okay. They just wanted to know what was wrong so they could help. But since Lyme disease is a complicated illness with many variations in symptom manifestation, how could a nine-year-old explain to her peers the medical dilemma that even doctors were struggling to decipher?

My daughter looked at me as if I were the Dalai Lama, having answers to all things on this plane of existence and beyond. Most people didn't realize that Lyme disease could be damaging to the extent that it can cause a person to stop being able to walk. It seemed that many people who had Lyme disease and were treated early had no symptoms of consequence. They were lucky. I recall a teacher or two telling me that they had been diagnosed with Lyme disease and that their primary symptoms were joint pain in the knees. The principal from Sophie's school told me that she had Ehrlichiosis, another tick-borne illness, but she must have been treated early enough, as she did not report symptoms similar to those that my daughter was experiencing. Most people spoke about Lyme disease as if it were a common occurrence that could be readily cured. Frankly, I thought to myself, they didn't have a clue as to what my daughter was suffering. There was so much more I didn't know. I had to keep searching.

Once I started to tell people about my daughter's illness, it seemed as if everyone had a story about Lyme disease. The people who got antibiotics early enough got well quickly. But those who never had the rash or never saw a tick were suffering in ways that I found astonishing. Some were sick for a long time and developed neurological diseases or autoimmune disorders that may have been related to Lyme disease. Some had co-infections and never seemed to get better. The list of complaints that people reported was like an endless array of stars in an infinite universe. It was frightening beyond belief. Lyme disease had taken the lives of many to a dark place. You could get help, but only if you had the money to pay for the doctors who would treat you, because insurance most often would not cover the cost of care. And there were so many variations in the way doctors treated these symptoms that it was difficult to figure out which protocol was the most effective. Diagnosis and treatment were still experimental. It was hard to imagine that people were getting sick and weren't able to access help.

For instance, there was the man who cleaned our gutters to whom my mother told Sophie's story. He explained that he had Lyme disease and had been on antibiotics for about nine months, and when he came off the antibiotics he would get ill and would have to go back on the medication to feel well. The man reported that he had developed depression from Lyme disease. He explained that he was married with children and had always been a relatively happy person, but all of a sudden, he would just start crying or withdraw for no apparent reason. He realized that it was all connected with Lyme disease. That was the first time I heard of Lyme disease being connected with psychiatric symptoms. The picture of what was happening to my daughter began to make more sense to me.

Then there was a mother who told the story of her daughter being so depressed that she was afraid to keep any items in the house that she could use to harm herself. She explained that she felt her daughter had to be watched, and missed an awful lot of school since she was so sad and depressed. Her friends didn't understand, and some of them lost interest in her daughter. I felt the sadness. It was the agony of not knowing what was to follow for her daughter and her family that was the collective pain we shared.

A coworker told me that her sister-in-law was telling her how her five-year-old nephew had started to become aggressive lately. He was having uncontrollable, angry outbursts. My coworker told her sister-in-law about my daughter and encouraged her to get her son tested for Lyme disease. A few days passed when my co-worker came to me and told me that her nephew had a positive test for Lyme disease and once he was put on medication, the outbursts ceased.

There was another situation that was brought to my attention. A mom I knew told me a story about her daughter who had started her second year at college away from home. She explained that suddenly her daughter was complaining of panic attacks. Her daughter had never had a problem with anxiety, she explained. Then she reported that she took her daughter to the doctor and that her daughter had undergone testing. I began to ask about her daughter's summer and what she did. The mother told me that her daughter spent time camping and being outdoors. I told her, "Listen, I know you'll probably think I'm crazy for telling you this, but make sure the doctor gives her a Lyme test." A few days passed and she called me. "Mindy, my daughter's Lyme test came back positive. She is now on medication and the panic attacks have stopped. Thank you so much. I would never have thought to have her tested for Lyme disease." We live in an endemic area, should testing for Lyme disease be part of an annual medical exam? When psychiatric symptoms emerge should doctors be looking for a medical explanation like the possibility that Lyme disease or other tickborne illnesses could be the cause?

I needed to hear all the stories I could. I felt as if each story had something in it for me, a message for my daughter. Each was a pathway of information leading to possible answers for how to get my daughter well. Also, as I listened to the various stories, I felt that I was no longer alone. There were clues in the stories that could help me figure out how things worked, clues that I needed to pay attention to for the sake of Sophie and my family. This was the most treacherous scavenger hunt of all time. I knew I just had to keep going, searching for clues, listening to each story, and learning about what other people did to get well—if they did get well.

It is dangerous to be right in matters on which the established authorities are wrong.

—Voltaire

About two weeks after we returned from the hospital, Sophie's father was nagging me to get a psychiatrist to see her. "Hey, if you want a psychiatrist, then you get one," I told him. I was just so mad at him. However, he persisted with selling this idea to me as if his life depended on it. We were not on the same plane of existence as far as Sophie was concerned. He believed that a psychiatrist would help our daughter get better. I wanted to run away from that idea as fast as I could. This was a medical issue and there was not one person who was going to convince me otherwise. He told me we should return to the psychologist who saw her at the hospital. For what reason, I did not know, but I was just too tired to fight, so I agreed to have Sophie go see the psychologist again as long as he made the appointment.

At first I had no plan of going to the appointment, but Sophie asked me to, so I willingly complied. Our other two daughters, Casey and Molly, joined as well. I knew they wanted to help their sister, but they felt lost too. Casey, my oldest daughter, was home on her college break. She was devoted to helping her sister in any way she could. Molly wanted to be there because we were a family that stuck together when stuff got bad, and this was bad, really bad. So off we went to the psychologist.

When we arrived at the office, the psychologist seemed delighted to see us. It was not a good time since Sophie had continued to have explosive outbursts and we were unable to control them. Her rage episodes were frightening exhibitions of burning anxiety, and lately they had become like a massive, out of control forest fire. She would move from one room to another, banging and slamming, running in circles, screaming and making deep, guttural, rasping sounds that were hair raising, bone chilling, and made my skin crawl. My daughter had become a lost child locked deep inside herself, in a place I was unable to reach into to pull her out. Sometimes, when she was out of control, her eyes were so dark and empty that I didn't know if she was still in there.

The psychologist summoned us into her office. Sitting in her wheelchair, Sophie rolled herself into the room. Then Peter, Casey, Molly, and I all sat down on a long sofa against the back wall of the office. Sophie sat in her wheelchair across the room from us, between the psychologist and the exit door. The psychologist began by asking Sophie how she was doing. Well, that was one provocative question, and Sophie was not going to be preyed upon. Sophie gave her a piece of her mind, with full awareness and intention. She gave the psychologist a dose of her pain. As I recall, the conversation proceeded in this manner. "Well, how do you think I am, sitting here in this wheelchair and you and the other doctors couldn't do anything for me?" The psychologist answered with, "Sophie, it sounds like you are in a great deal of pain." Sophie turned her wheelchair away from the psychologist and looked at the wall. "What do you know about my pain? What do you know about anything?" she said. "You could not help then, you can't help me now."

Although it was heart wrenching to watch Sophie say these things, I must admit that I felt gratified and proud. I was seeing that my little girl had the guts to tell this woman, this psychologist, what she thought of her and her expertise. "You don't know anything," Sophie told her, while moving closer to the wall to bang her wheelchair right into it over and over again. We all sat quietly on the long sofa watching this scene. Sophie yelled at the psychologist about how she felt.

"I'm in this wheelchair and I don't know if I will ever get out of it. That is how I feel. You did not help me, can't you see that I am unable to walk?" she yelled as she continued to bang her wheelchair into the wall.

"So you think that this is related to an unresolved medical issue," the psychologist replied looking at Peter, Casey, Molly, and I. What do you think we have been saying all along. Are you oblivious to my daughter's predicament?

"Well I don't think you can take her home like this. I am going to call next door to the psychiatric unit and see whether they can meet with you today." Here we go again. This is what Peter wanted so I was going to go along for the ride and see what happened.

It was agonizing to watch Sophie go through this episode, but somehow I knew that she was getting her anger out, releasing the bottled-up feelings she had about not being able to walk, doctors not knowing what to do, and being so helpless. I was drained, but grateful for the catharsis that was happening for my little girl. I lived the anger right there with her and felt it being drawn out of me. I was hanging on to Sophie's strength that she spat out like venom over the person that was the mirror of powerlessness for her.

The psychologist recommended that we hospitalize Sophie in a children's psychiatric unit and referred us to where the children were admitted.

So together we went to have Sophie evaluated for admission into a children's psychiatric unit, like zombies. We were greeted by a young woman who took down the essential facts and insurance data. Then Sophie, Peter, and I were escorted into a room to wait for the team to arrive to assess her. Casey and Molly went to get a bite to eat. Sophie had a worried look upon her face. I felt like getting up and leaving to go home, but I sat waiting, paralyzed. I knew there were no answers here, but for Peter's sake, I sat and waited, feeling like an outsider looking in. Three people walked into the room: the social worker, the assistant, and the psychiatrist. The psychiatrist was friendly, asking Sophie lots of questions that we assisted in answering along the way. Mostly we were quiet while Sophie spoke in a soft, sad voice. When all was said and done, they left the room. I asked Peter what he thought, and he replied, "We are not leaving her here." Relief radiated through me. I wanted to cheer and scream for joy that we were taking our baby girl home and out of this godforsaken institution. I loved that he wasn't a total believer in what they were saying and doing. The tables were turning for him, I hoped, because I needed him to be brave for Sophie and our family.

It is not ignorance but knowledge which is the mother of wonder.

—Joseph Wood Krutch

The Psychiatrist Visit

After we got home from the unsuccessful attempt of others to place my daughter in a psychiatric hospital, we relaxed, knowing that hospitalization was not the path we were going to take. Relieved that I had overcome Peter's persistence to see where the psychologist was taking us, I could bask in the glory that her voice no longer had a place in our lives. I was ready to try to locate a psychiatrist who might be able to prescribe medication to help my daughter with these episodes of rage. I was not very confident that her symptoms could be managed in this way, but nevertheless I was ready to try it. We found a local psychiatrist who could see Sophie quickly.

Together, Sophie, her father, and I went to the psychiatrist's office and sat in the waiting room looking at the unhappy faces, anxiously waiting to be called. In the psychiatrist's office we begin to tell Sophie's story—the most abbreviated version we could muster up for this visit, knowing that time was limited. We focused on her uncontrollable rage outbursts. Due to the agitation we had noted during these outbursts, Sophie was diagnosed with anxiety. The psychiatrist, who mostly treated children, talked about how Sophie's anxiety manifested into these outbursts. Of course, as a mental health practitioner, I found nothing new in this, only the fact that it was my daughter we were discussing, not another child. The psychiatrist was cautious in her prescribing practices, which fit well with my view that we should be careful about giving Sophie psychotropic medication due to the fact that bacteria was causing the neurological disturbance.

After the interview and a discussion of the current symptoms, we agreed to try a low dose of Prozac, which we hoped would prevent the agitation that led to the explosive rage outbursts.

The visit ended and we were left holding a prescription that we hoped would be the key to some stability and normalcy in our lives. The Prozac appeared to be helpful for about five months. It did not stop the rage episodes or eliminate them, but it did seem to reduce their frequency. The explosive outbursts that had been occurring several times a week were now happening once a week or once every other week. What was reducing these rage episodes was hard to determine. It was not clear whether she was just getting better from the antibiotic or whether the Prozac was reducing the frequency of the outbursts.

Once the Prozac had run its course, over about six months, and was no longer effective, we tried Abilify for about two weeks, which increasingly agitated Sophie, and then Risperdal for a couple of days, which resulted in more adverse side effects. It was at this point in time that we decided that psychotropic medications were not going to help Sophie and stopped them completely.

A taste for truth at any cost is a passion which spares nothing.

—Albert Camus

About two weeks after returning from the hospital Peter threw another recommendation at me.

"Let's go back to the neurologist," he said.

"What would we do that for?" I asked.

"Well, maybe he can give us some more information on what is happening to Sophie since the hospital wasn't able to do anything."

"What makes you think he knows what to do?"

"I don't know if he will be able to do anything for her, but at least we can go over what has happened so far and see if he has any suggestions."

"Okay," I responded. I guessed it couldn't hurt any to go back to the neurologist since we were making a return visit to other doctors as well. The following day I set up the appointment.

Luckily, I was able to schedule the neurologist quickly. A few days later, Sophie and I found ourselves at the neurologist's office waiting for the doctor. Peter was supposed to meet us there, but we had been called into the exam room before he arrived. Again we were seen by the nurse practitioner, who told us that the doctor from the hospital had called the neurologist and was quite upset that he had diagnosed Sophie with Lyme disease. I was totally shocked by this disclosure. I had stumbled upon some secret information without even trying. I felt betrayed by the doctors, who were mad at each other while my daughter was still unable to walk because they disagreed on the diagnosis of Lyme disease. What about the truth? Didn't anyone out there care about the truth? I couldn't believe that this was the reality I was living.

The doctor walked in and I told him about the hospital ordeal. He listened as he looked at my daughter and then began the same neurological exam he had performed daily in the hospital, forcing her to step out of the wheelchair and walk. I wanted to scream, "What the hell are you doing?"

"Come on," he said to Sophie. "Get up and walk, bend your legs."

She tried hard to walk but she was unable to move her legs. She leaned against the exam table and once again, just like in the hospital, she collapsed against the doctor who was standing right in front of her. He sat her back in the wheelchair. I was flabbergasted seeing my child tortured like this, and yet I wasn't doing a damn thing about it. What kind of mother was I? I was unable to fathom my own response to this madness. The conversation with the neurologist, as I recall it, progressed in this way: "She can't walk," I said.

"I can see that," he said.

"Is there anything else that can be done?"

"Well, we can do a lumbar puncture."

"You mean a spinal tap?"

"Yes, a lumbar puncture."

"I don't think there is any proof that a spinal tap will tell if she has Lyme disease."

"Well, if you want to know for sure, then you have to do the lumbar puncture."

Had this doctor heard what I had just said? No, I didn't think so. So back and forth we went, with him insisting that a lumbar puncture was the confirmatory test and me telling him that it was too risky and that I was not putting her through that pain. Finally I told him that I was not doing that test and that it was time for us to leave. I pushed Sophie's wheelchair out of the room, thoroughly exasperated. I wanted to yell out, "Does anyone know what they are doing?" Just as I was leaving the exam room with my daughter, Peter arrived.

About a year later, I returned to the neurologist to show him that Sophie was getting better. I told him how long she had been on antibiotics and he said that it was a long time to be on antibiotics. He said that it was good to see her getting better, but there was no acknowledgement about what he may have missed or the fact that I had been right. I didn't need his validation, but I wanted him to know that she was getting better without him.

Furthermore, I wanted him to know that he had been right about her having Lyme disease but wrong about the spinal tap. I guess that he hadn't known what to do about the Lyme disease, and that saddened me. How many others had crossed his path and gone away empty handed?

You cannot create experience. You must undergo it.

—Albert Camus

About ten weeks into the doxycycline regimen, Sophie was still showing improvements, but still had severe sound sensitivity, so we had to walk on eggshells around the house. We were still going for physical therapy, which had been going well. I sat and watched as the therapist took her through the exercises and then held her while she walked the length of the office. Sophie was walking pretty well, as she had been practicing balance exercises over the last few weeks. I was so excited I went over to her and asked her if she wanted to continue walking back and forth in the office. She did. I held her elbow while we took steps slowly to the end of the office where the chairs sat for waiting patients. Then we turned around and walked back toward the smaller, individual offices with tables for other exercises. She seemed excited too, as she was becoming more confident about her walking and balance. Then it was time to go home.

When we got home, Sophie asked if I could hold her so she could continue walking. She walked the path up to the house as I held her elbow. Then she walked with me just holding her hand. She felt like she was getting the walking, like a child learning to take her first confident steps. I kept spurring her on until finally I let her go. She kept walking on her own without realizing it until she turned to look back at me a few steps behind her. It was like when a child is learning to ride a bicycle without training wheels, and is let go by the parent only to discover that she is riding on her own. Sophie's face lit up and tears filled my eyes as she screamed out to me, "Mommy, Mommy, look, it's a miracle, it's a miracle, I can walk!"

She was so surprised that she was able to walk that she could not stop walking. It was as if she was afraid that the ability to walk would disappear as quickly as it arrived. She went into the house to share her miracle with the family.

I could see Peter looking surprised and relieved. He had thought she would not be able to walk again, but faith had brought me comfort, and my daughter's progress had assured me that I was moving in the right direction. Sophie's progress that day reignited my perseverance with a vengeance. It was the first day in a long time that I saw a small smile on her face—a piece of joy that transformed her despair into believing that just maybe she could get better. As Sophie toyed with the idea that walking could make all the painful horror go away, I thought about how many steps there were on the road to getting well. I felt as if I was hanging on the precipice of a cliff. I needed to wither away hopeless thoughts, fight hard, and push forward because I could now see there was a light at the end of the tunnel—and Sophie was walking toward it.

Optimism is the madness of insisting that all is well when we are miserable.

—Voltaire

Two Steps Forward, One Step Back

By four months into the doxycycline regimen, Sophie had made massive improvements in her walking and overall physical activity. After the physical therapy ended we began yoga to further strengthening her legs. For the first time since before she had gotten sick, I saw her do a cartwheel and a handstand right there on the living room floor. It reminded me of the days prior to her illness when she attended gymnastics. Sophie had loved to practice her cartwheels and handstands anywhere there was space in the house. Outside in the yard, I would always caution her not to do these stunts on the concrete for fear of injury to her head, neck, or spine.

Sophie was accustomed to having the freedom to express herself. An overwhelming joy came along with that freedom. A milestone had been reached. Her smile wrapped itself around me like a gigantic hug as I watched her twirl around the front yard. I had hoped to see this moment, and here it was, before my eyes. A smiling, happy child was before me. I once again had a glimpse into the person Sophie had been prior to her being ill and not the psychotic-looking, feral child who had been a raging stranger to me. My child had returned to show me that she was still there. Her progress was now the motivation I needed to keep going forward. Hope had emerged from the quagmire of despair.

Bedtime was approaching and I asked Sophie whether she had taken her medication. "No, Mom," she said. "I forgot to take it." So I gave her the medication and told her to get ready for bed. About fifteen or so minutes had passed before she came into my room screaming, "Mommy, I'm scared, I see people trying to kill you and Daddy, it's so scary." She let out a squeal that sounded like a piece of metal being dragged down a blackboard and I shivered. It's another rage episode fueled by anxiety, creating a menace of magnified fear inside her head. I took her into her room and lay down with her on her bed, holding her close. She clung to me, squeezing so tight as if a monster of epic proportions was grabbing at her back. I held her close, telling her over and over again it would be okay, that I was there and I would protect her. She stared at me with frightened eyes and I knew that in her mind she was running. Her breathing was rapid and she gasped for breath as she screamed, shutting her eyes as if to shut out the nightmare facing her.

Sophie screamed about what she saw in her mind for about twenty minutes. I could barely get through this episode, but giving up was not an option. Then she tried hard to give me a clue as to how I could help her. She asked me to talk about something else to distract her from the "bad thoughts," as she described them. This was something new: Sophie was trying to help herself get control. Maybe she was beginning to feel like she had the power to control these awful, horrifying thoughts. I told her that I would try to distract her. I started by talking about the new musical theater day camp that she would be attending, and I kept on talking as I watched her eyes following the words coming out of my mouth. She was hanging onto every syllable as if her life depended on it to calm her brain. The words flowed freely as I told her that she would meet new friends, learn how to act, and create scenery. Sophie told me that she knew there would be a show at the end of the week. She wondered what show they would pick to do. Back and forth we went, talking our way into the world of tomorrow and what might be. Slowly, it seemed to be working. She held onto me as the fear was beginning to dissipate. Maybe she had found a way out of the madness that was trying to take hold of her mind. She seemed to have found a path within the maze that could lead to a way out. Now she was able to tell me what I could do to help her. Now I had a clue as to how to help her. She was stronger now, and able to try harder to push the bad thoughts out of her mind. It was a key to hold onto that opened the door to new possibilities. Even if we were not sure what exactly was making her feel stronger inside. Had the antibiotics reached into her brain to attack the bacteria that had been igniting her synapses?

I realized that I had to find some medication to help Sophie calm down. As a mental health professional who has worked in residential treatment centers serving children and adolescents for many years, I knew that Benadryl was often used to calm down out-of-control kids. It magically sedated the young person until communication could occur that would resolve the episode. So Benadryl was my solution for my daughter.

As time went on I got more familiar with how the rage episodes would emerge, and I would give Sophie a single dose of the liquid form of Benadryl because it worked faster. It took about fifteen minutes for it to take effect and it would calm her down so she could fall asleep. Once she awoke after the episode had passed, I would see calm in her eyes and I would know she felt slightly better. Sophie did not like taking so many medications and supplements. It reminded her of what was happening to her, and she would avoid it any way she could—pushing it out of her mind even if only temporarily.

Benadryl was a good choice: quick and effective, with little to no side effects for the desired result. It was also more successful than Ativan, which had turned out to be an ineffective solution. My experience had helped me to see a way out for my daughter, and I was taking it.

Sweet is the voice of a sister in the season of sorrow.

—Benjamin Disraeli

I'm not your average nosy mother, but one day during the afternoon when Sophie and her sister Casey were out in the backyard, I strolled into Sophie's room to straighten things up. That was my usual way—I would walk through the house looking for items that were out of place and put them where they belonged, trying to bring some semblance of order to my home. My daughter Casey had left her laptop sitting open on her bed. I picked it up, sat down, and placed it on my lap. Then it happened: I started to look at what was on the screen. There was an email to her boyfriend, and my curiosity got the best of me. I began reading it.

It's 8:15am on Thursday morning...I went to go to the bathroom but Sophie was in there and by acci-

dent I stepped on her foot cuz when I just wake up I'm still asleep and my eyes aren't fully open lol…but she started screaming bloody murder cuz I guess her muscles still bother her if you do anything to them even by accident and I started apologizing but at first she said get away from me and I tried to help but she just wouldn't listen but then my mom talked to her and she forgave me… but little things like that suck… well of course my parents yell at me I mean mostly my Dad…how could you be such an idiot blah blah blah… of course I wasn't being an idiot I was just being clumsy but sometimes you can't help things like that… I guess I just have to watch where I go… she's a small person, of course I feel bad. I miss you.

I scrolled down, looking at a few prior emails, and continued to read about how Casey's summer was going, but her emails weren't happy and it hurt me to think that I had stopped her from having fun by asking her to watch her sister. Was it right to ask her to help out?

So we just came home from the library after being there for about an hour cuz Sophie's arms started burning cuz they got burnt…I guess her medicine does really affect her being in the sun no matter how much sunscreen she puts on…I hate it…it's not fair that this had to happen to her ughh and I haven't eaten anything since breakfast because I lost my appetite because of everything that happened today but now I'm starved… I miss you more than you know.

I peeked into the hallway to see if anyone was lurking around and decided I would read just one more email. I scurried back to the bed and looked again at the screen.

You won't believe what has happened since the last time I emailed you...well, everything was going well...I got Sophie off the bus and she went swimming while I laid out in the sun...then awhile later she was complaining that her cheeks were burning so I put on more sunscreen but it made things worse because it started to sting... and Sophie really can't handle the pain cause of all she has been through so we went right inside the house and Sophie began going crazy, throwing everything around...ripping papers... hitting and scratching and punching me and Molly for about 30 min...she scratched me till I was bleeding because I can't fight back...I can push her away but let me tell you she is one strong little girl...I called my mom right away but it took her about 20 to 25 minutes to get home and she didn't stop till my mom got home and helped calm her down... Molly and I cleaned up the whole mess...Anyway, any little pain is so much worse for Sophie...I feel bad cause I can't help her feel better and all she wants is my mom... I miss you so much.

Casey had sacrificed her first summer after graduating from college to come home for Sophie. Although it was a challenge to figure out how to handle Sophie's random explosions, Casey would not let her sister down. She wanted to help her sister just like we all did.

Reading Casey's thoughts in those emails made me wonder how many more there were that told the story of Sophie's illness and her sisters' struggle to help, feeling useless. I was amazed that she was able to stay home, help her sister, and give back to her family. It was the way I always thought it should be and so I was proud that Casey was able to do the giving.

Most of the time while Casey watched over Sophie, they played indoors, because exposure to the sun was a contraindication of doxycycline. Although this frustrated Sophie, Casey made her sister's life bearable by staying with her and helping to comfort and entertain her. Sophie often did not want to be around friends, as she did not want anyone to see her in her condition. She was struggling with her own ability to cope with the changes she faced and the horror her life had become. The last thing she wanted was for one of her peers to see how she was and not be able to explain it.

When Sophie did feel better she tried to connect with her peers, but this was also a challenge. She just didn't feel good most of the time and never wanted to spoil the fun for other kids. Sophie would not verbalize this to anyone but me. When we spent time together Sophie shared what was happening to her and whom she felt comfortable being around. Sophie always told me she wanted her sisters to be there for her because she felt safe and secure with them. Their love was unconditional and that was most important in a time of sorrow and uncertainty.

Molly enjoyed taking Sophie out when she was feeling good. Together they would go see a movie or go shopping. Sophie was desperate to enjoy every good moment she could absorb in a day and having her sister take her out were times when she had a great deal of fun and took her mind away from what her life had become. Since Casey and Molly were older, they could drive and go places a younger sister would not have been able to offer. Sophie took all the joy that was possible from each and every interaction with her sisters. They provided her with as much as they could give, knowing that the unpredictable elements of her illness could put a damper on their activities outside of the house. Her sisters wanted to be there for her, but sometimes weren't sure what to do to make her feel better. Attempting to understand the mountain that we had to climb to get to a better place was like a mathematical equation yet to be solved. Molly was frustrated, as I focused on Sophie all the time, but continued to give what she could to her sister. Casey left for graduate school feeling guilty that she could not be there to help her sister. But I did not uncover the magnitude of their secret struggles until much later.

Not being able to anticipate what would happen next was the worst part of our existence. The illness had us walking a tightrope. Although we were all agonized by the unexpected results of the illness, Sophie's sisters were able to continue giving their unconditional love and support to their little sister. The bond of sisterly love kept them holding onto one another for strength.

Words have no power to impress
the mind without the exquisite
horror of their reality.

—Edgar Allan Poe

School

One of the days I lay in bed with Sophie, she had told me about school and what making the transition from the wheelchair to walking had been like. Sophie said that the people she had thought were her friends weren't real. I asked her, "What do you mean?" Sophie looked away as she described the way all the students in the class helped her when she was in the wheelchair even though they never really understood why she was in the wheelchair, but once she was out of it, they all assumed she was fine and ignored her. Their understanding of Lyme disease or any disease process was limited as their youthfulness was a natural deterrent to grasping such complexities of life. Her sad face reminded me of a wilted flower and brought a flood of tears to my eyes.

Sophie continued to look away as she described the way in which her classmates had left her destitute without her wheelchair. "Were they real?" she asked me. She said she felt like she was invisible. She craved some acknowledgement of the kindnesses that had been extended to her while she was helpless in the wheelchair.

Now that Sophie was walking, she felt bereft, without the hope of a kind word ever reaching her ears. Her proud achievement was now her social failure. Her peers had gladly returned to their small groups of friends within the classroom. They did not intend to hurt her, only to restore the equilibrium that was their life. Yet their wordless judgments were stinging to Sophie. Their behavior toward her while she was in the wheelchair was a false kindness pushed upon them to treat those less fortunate with a helping hand, she felt. Sophie believed that their friendship had been a temporary measure called for by their teacher. The reality, that it had merely been a short-lived façade, tore at the very core of her being. "Why are they like this?" she asked me. I was lost as to how I could possibly answer as to how the world worked—and how people worked the world. It was something no child should have to encounter at such a tender age. I suppose there isn't a person out there in the world that should have to suffer the feeling that is attached to being proclaimed invisible in the social arena regardless of the reason.

Sophie told me about a teacher's assistant who had helped her when she was in the wheelchair to take the elevator to the second floor to her class. Once inside the elevator, the woman would ask her questions about her weekend. Sophie would reply with the mundane details of the events that consumed her life over the two days between school days. Then Sophie described what this woman had meant to her. "This woman, you know, she was my only companion. She listened to me."

How Sophie was able to see inside her situation in such a profound manner overwhelmed me with emotion. She was able to get to the heart of the matter in a few short words as to the predicament of her illness. She was like a wounded animal in a barren land and this woman was her savior. But even more important than that was Sophie's acknowledgement that this woman was a gift that had been given to her. Sometimes when Sophie entered school in the wheelchair this woman would ask, according to Sophie's recollection, "So are you ready to race?" Sophie would smile and then the two of them would secretly race down the hallway to the elevator with Sophie maneuvering the wheelchair down the hallway while the woman jogged right alongside her. It was fun for Sophie, probably the only fun she could squeeze out of her day at that time. Sophie just wanted her life to be the way it was before Lyme disease hit, but she was far away from the vision she had held of her life before this tragic event. Lyme disease had changed her world and how she saw it. There was no coming back from that. Her experience had made her different. When something happens to you, it changes who you are. You don't go back to being the person you were before. It just doesn't work that way. A deep sadness poured over me like a waterfall. Would she ever get to a place of happiness again?

Nothing can make injustice just but mercy.

—Robert Frost

Lyme Rage, Part III

The next day Sophie entertained herself in her room all day because she couldn't be out in the sun due to the doxycycline. By evening she was laughing and running around the house with her sisters. She seemed to be quite hyper, which was not usual for her—although there was nothing usual about Lyme disease. I could hear Sophie's sisters telling her that it was time to go to bed, so I looked at the clock and saw that it was already eleven p.m.

Sophie was usually in bed by this time but she had been having such fun with her sisters that I did not have the heart to stop her. It was summer and her sister Casey had returned from college, so all three girls had time together. But soon I could hear that the frivolity and fun were over, so I got out of bed to see what was happening. Sophie was unable to sit calmly or lie down because she was too hyper. She was able to tell me what was happening to her. She explained that she was unable to calm herself and I realized this could be the start of a rage episode. Before I was able to think about what to do next, Sophie started screaming, running around the house in circles. Her father came out of the bedroom and told her, "Sophie cut it out." He then walked away back into the bedroom. As he was walking away, Sophie said, "I can't control it," but he didn't hear her. Sophie continued to scream and run. I tried to get a glimpse of her eyes, which would tell me how far away she might be. There was something inside of her pulling her away and I didn't know if I could hold on to her. I stood and watched as she ran around in circles, her feet hitting the floor and pounding away as if she were pulling a ball and chain with her.

I was trying to figure out whether to jump in and get Sophie to her room or let it take its course. I was the one who would decide what we would do next. Everybody was waiting for my signal as to which switch would get pulled or pushed into action. I decided to get Sophie to go into her room. As we walked together down the hallway, Sophie told me, "Mommy, I can't stop the screaming in my head. Mommy, I can't stop it, I can't stop it." The panic in her voice sent a shiver right through me. I lay down next to her on her bed and held her tight in my arms. She squeezed me with enormous strength, her arms around my neck. I kept telling her that it would be okay, that it would soon stop if she could try and relax. I told her that I knew it was hard for her to stop it, and I knew that she couldn't control it, but that I also knew that there would be an end to it. I kept telling her that it would stop.

Gradually, Sophie calmed down on her own. The episode slowed and, like a train, came to a halt, and she was out of it, this time without Benadryl. When she started talking to me like a normal nine-year-old child again, I knew we had made it through another episode without incident. What a relief. I could now rest and go to sleep.

I only hoped that I would be able to head off the next episode before it hit like a train wreck.

I needed to conjure up a plan—a logical, organized way of predicting when another rage episode would occur—so that I, the almighty mother, could prevent this awful thing from taking over Sophie again. That was an image that I had created for myself to cope with these unpredictable episodes of Sophie's mind being held hostage by Lyme disease's bacterial invasion. I could envision the snakelike flagella swimming around in her head, wreaking so much havoc with her mind that it short-circuited into madness for brief periods. Could I ever find the way to getting her better? I still didn't know the answer to this question, so all I could do was to keep going, hoping that I would stumble upon it. My mission was to keep following the path to wellness. That was all I could do—just follow the path until there was an end if that was even possible. And I knew that I would have to walk it alone. My acceptance of this reality kept me pragmatic and persevering.

Five months into the doxycycline regimen, if there was any progress that could in any way be quantified as such, it was very slow. Sophie's body was only incrementally recognizing the foreign invader that had devoured her. Some mornings I would awaken feeling sick to my stomach. I would look at myself in the mirror in my bathroom and see yet again darkness under my eyes. Feeling like the life had been sucked right out of me, my life was like a well that had run dry. I felt thirsty and my mouth was parched. I stared into space, seeking a sign, a symbol of hope, something to kick me into start mode, but it was useless. Every day was the same. Every setback had me falling back into a pit of hopelessness. Just when I thought that my baby girl was getting better, I would put her to sleep at night only to reawaken to her nightmare in the morning—if we were lucky enough to sleep through the night at all.

After sleeping for about fifteen minutes on that particular night Sophie started screaming. When I went to her, she had the eyes of a stranger once again, with a dark, faraway gaze. She was unable to speak about what was happening to her, but I knew. It was Lyme disease tapping the inner workings of her brain, releasing anxiety at levels beyond human tolerance. The rage enveloped her into a cocoon and she was desperately holding on to her sanity. That evil little spirochete was wrecking her mind again. Sophie was unable to stop screaming. She was so loud that hearing her voice meant feeling intolerable pain. Soon she was panting with anxiety, gasping for air. Yet she was lying next to me and I was holding her tight. I told her as I always did, "It's going to be okay." But that didn't matter, because for her it was anything but okay and might never be okay. I knew it, she knew it, and I was lost, floundering like a fish out of water. I kept repeating the same thing over and over again, as if that would make it all right. I knew it was a lie but I kept doing it, programmed by the false idea that it was comforting to her. I wanted to believe that I could make it okay. What else was there for me to do to help eradicate the horror that smacked her brain over and over again? I hugged her tight so she knew that I was in it with her, wherever it was that we were traveling. She knew that I hung on the edge of the precipice with her, that she was not alone.

I realized I needed to give her Benadryl so I told her I had to get up to go get it, but she looked at me with terror in her eyes, so we got up together, without me letting go of her, our arms locked around each other. Standing, she hid her head against me like a shy child, and she was shaking with fear. Together we went into the kitchen to get the Benadryl. I picked up the plastic, single-dose vial as she clung to me, and got the scissors to cut it open. The whole time she was hanging onto me as if I were her lifeline. In some ways, I suppose I was her lifeline because I provided the safety she needed to survive this treacherous illness.

We walked back to her room after she had swallowed the Benadryl. Sophie continued to scream. I watched as she twisted and turned on her bed, writhing to get the thoughts to leave her body. Staring into her empty eyes, I told her I knew that she was here with me and all would be okay. She looked my way for a fraction of a second in silent acknowledgement that she was with me. Then a screech passed right through me. I sat down on her bed and grabbed hold of her as she let out these short bursts of sound. Sophie gripped my arms like a vice and held onto me so that the fear did not pull her under. She was gasping for breath as another terrifying thought hit, sending a shock wave through her body. I knew she saw death and killing in her mind. "Bad things," she would call them, afraid to tell me of the thoughts whirling around in her head. She was not calming down so quickly this time, so I decided to take her out of her room and into my bedroom, hoping that the change would help dissipate the vivid thought pattern of death at her doorstep. Sophie's father was watching television as we entered the room. As we got into bed he shut off the television and the lights. Sophie screamed so loud the vibration hurt my eardrums. I turned the light back on. Darkness was no longer tolerable for Sophie during these episodes. The light gave her some connection to reality.

I held her until the Benadryl took over and she could no longer keep her eyes open. About forty-five minutes had passed. Now Sophie was peacefully sleeping. Her father and I lay in bed like two dead bodies—so serene, yet so drained. Once again, it felt as if our life force had been sucked right out of us without warning.

A mass murder had been committed in the mind of a child while she hid in a corner watching her own thoughts, fretful that the dream would capture her. All I wanted was to wash it all away with tears of love and compassion. I pleaded to a higher order for mercy in the name of my child.

When you have a sick child, you think only of them and what you can do to bring the smallest measure of peace and comfort to them. Your body acts like a programmed robot, moving with your child, following their direction, hanging onto a fragile existence.

I tried to get some sleep, but it was useless. My thoughts were traveling at warp speed. Twisting and turning, pulling the sheets out of their fitted place on the bed, I was restless and writhing with powerlessness. I feared that the path I was traveling was doomed. Finally, sleep overtook me and my thoughts drowned in its deep, dark, calm ocean.

Morning came too soon and the events of the night before haunted me in the light of day. Again, I felt sick to my stomach. In the mirror over the sink in my bathroom, I looked like a stranger to myself as my owl eyes stared back at me. Could I cope with these unexpected episodes of rage that had fallen upon us like a tornado, unleashing nature's fury in Sophie's path? I reminded myself that Lyme treatment is not a linear progression. I had to acknowledge that there was nothing linear here. Lyme disease is a deviant invader with an endless puzzle of symptoms that keep reemerging. There were no assurances for total recovery.

I am above the weakness of
seeking to establish a sequence
of cause and effect, between the
disaster and atrocity.

—Edgar Allan Poe

More Lyme Symptoms

After a little more than six months had passed, Sophie appeared to be doing better. She was going to school, doing her homework, and coping better with conflicts. Although she still got agitated easily, she calmed down quicker, so it seemed more manageable. But we were also accustomed to the situation and the rage episodes so we had adjusted to her behaviors. As a result, we had come to expect them as part of the normal order of things.

Sophie had also returned to many of her activities like voice lessons. One week she was home studying for a test at school, and I was in a rush as usual before we left for her lesson. "We must hurry," I told her, "so we won't be late." Sophie got her notebook and we went out to the car and had a snack on the way.

Upon arrival, the teacher was delighted to see us since Sophie had not been there for a lesson for a while. She asked Sophie how she was doing and what song she was interested in working on. Sophie began by talking about her day and everything appeared to be going well. She chose a song by Selena Gomez, her idol. I watched her start to sing but was monitoring the situation carefully as I knew that any change could trigger a volcanic eruption. I noticed that she was looking slightly pale and faint. Then she started to look at me with the telepathic message in her eyes that told me something was about to go awfully wrong. Suddenly she stopped singing. The teacher asked her what was wrong and she said her face felt hot and her chest was tightening. She was offered some water, which she took gratefully and began to drink.

By then I was watching her like a hawk. I knew that something was really wrong and told the teacher that we would need to stop the lesson. I told Sophie that we were leaving as I could sense a disaster approaching. We all began to walk out of the room into the waiting area and Sophie collapsed to the floor as if having a seizure. I grabbed her just in time so that her head did not hit the ground. Her body was deadweight in my arms as I tried to pull her up on to the sofa. I was unable to get her up so she lay there on the floor with her eyes closed, then opened them slightly and stared blankly, as if she were in a trance. I was talking to her, asking her to try to get up. I knew that she could hear me because her eyelashes fluttered, but she was unable to move.

Was she having a seizure? I was not sure what it was, but it looked like a seizure. I was lost as to do next. I couldn't make sense out of what was happening. I was unable to think yet I knew I must move to action. The teacher looked lost too as she watched what was happening to Sophie, wanting to help. Then everything clicked and I moved into action mode. I told her it was okay and I would get Sophie to the car. Again, I asked for Sophie's help and slowly she recognized me as if she had awakened from a deep sleep. I got her up and held her around the waist as I directed her to walk. We got to the car and I put her in the back seat and she collapsed. She lay lifeless as I turned on the ignition.

As soon as we reached the end of the driveway, she started kicking the window with her feet and thrashing around, but I was unable to stop, as I needed to get her home—and quickly. I talked to her while she was screaming, kicking with her arms flailing all over the back seat. "Hold my hand," I told her as I drove the car with one arm. She was screaming, telling me that something was inside of her and she could feel it. I wished I could pull that thing out of her. I was tortured by the feeling of helplessness. Seeing her struggling to grasp the handle of the roller coaster that was taking her for a ride to the edge once again, I was stunned into silence. We were only twenty minutes from home but it felt like a ride through the darkest tunnel filled with evildoers. What was happening to my little girl? Was it a seizure of some sort? There was nothing I could do to stop it or slow it down. It had to follow its path until whatever it was that was inside of her subsided. Lyme disease was the menace that was not only taking over her body, but also attacking her mind.

By the time we were almost at the front door of the house she was calmer. It was as if whatever had taken over her body had now left and she was back to being herself. But for me it was not over. I felt my throat closing up and I was gasping for air. I wanted to run away and never look back. I wanted to escape this awful feeling of impending doom as my cup runneth over with dreadfulness. I feared that she wouldn't be well again and I would be subjected to more of these unpredictable episodes of rage, seizures, and whatever else came from the bacteria tormenting her body. I would have to tolerate the helplessness over and over again. There may be periods of relief, but there would always be the unpredictability that out of nowhere I would be struck by helplessness. This unplanned event would take all the goodness away from me. A stolen moment of joy would be whisked away and only blackness would survive which would swallow me up. It would haunt me like a ghost haunts a child. I would want to run away and never turn back. I was unable to surrender to this desire, as my little girl needed me. I was coherent yet paralyzed. I knew that these episodes were not happening as frequently, but the element of not knowing when they would occur was exhausting, debilitating. Although she seemed to recover untouched by the monster that had ruthlessly taken over her body and mind, I was weighed down by the event. I was being squeezed thoroughly, wrung out like a rag thrown into a bucket after wiping up messy glop. My confidence felt like the Titanic—it was a sinking ship. I needed to hold on to a piece of hope, as if I were digging for a lost treasure.

About seven or so months along on the antibiotic regimen, Sophie was attending full days of school and there seemed to be more days that she was able and functional. Then I got a call from the nurse who told me that Sophie was sitting in her office with her sweatshirt pulled over her face. I knew immediately that she was trying to control the rage budding as the anxiety traveled through her bloodstream. There was no trigger to be sure of in any of these events, but when they erupted I had to get her out of wherever she was and get her home.

Sophie's embarrassment was not to be taken lightly. She had been humiliated by the disease, which took her dignity from her and disposed of it. I told the nurse without hesitation that I would come and get her.

Then I explained to everyone at home what was happening. I always had to explain to the people in my family what was happening to Sophie, as if I were the interpreter of events. It was as if she were an alien from another planet and only I had been given the secret code to interpret her telepathic communication. As I quickly hopped into my car and sped down the road to the school, I felt my adrenaline pumping. I had no time to think because my mind was filled with the picture of the road in front of me. I got there in record time and was buzzed into the school by the secretary. Sophie had been sitting in the nurse's office. The nurse was one of the kindest women I knew and one of the most compassionate as well. I was grateful for her being the savior for my daughter at school. However, the nurse slowly broke the news to me as my daughter sat in the corner, her arms wrapped around herself, looking at me. Sophie had gotten upset and thrown a chair at her. The chair had not hit her and she was okay. I was shocked. Sophie's stare told me that she had lost control but that she was contrite. The nurse kept on talking and I faded away into my daughter's face. Dazed, I was brought back to life with the notion that I had to get Sophie home where I could help her best.

Despite popular opinion, I knew that it was the Lyme that was making her agitated, aggressive, and full of paranoid terror. Others were unable to fathom that Lyme disease could do this to a person. There was no imagination that could conjure up how such changes could alter a person's character. There was no way to mimic the sound that emerged from Sophie when she was in a state of near madness. I felt like I was left with my head in a vice that was being squeezed by the denial of my family and their belief that this was some made-up fairytale gone wrong. The pain was too great and the difference in Sophie was too severe for me to tolerate the evisceration of the little girl who was our daughter. There was no quick fix here.

Only those who will risk going too far can possibly find out how far one can go.

—T.S. Eliot

Another visit to Dr. Cameron revealed that Sophie may have reached a plateau, and Sophie's father was less than satisfied with her progress over the past eight months or so. This triggered a discussion of cause and effect, expert opinions, getting his daughter well, and which path had the quickest outcome. So Dr. Cameron discussed with us trying another medication, Cefta, with the hope that this would further her progress. We left the office and went out to the reception desk to pay the bill. The friendly support staff at the doctor's office appeared genuinely surprised by Sophie's progress. They reminded me of how far she had come.

We left the office and got into the car to drive home as quickly as possible so we could fill the prescription. Hopefully, this step would lead us closer to our destination. It was frightening, as we did not know what would come next. Would Cefta be the answer we had been waiting for or would it push us off a cliff to fall screaming downward with no safety net?

That night it was time for Sophie to take the new medication. She was given it as usual, but there was nothing usual about our expectations or our desire to crawl out of the medieval torture chamber that seemed to be holding us hostage. Sophie was quiet all night until the next morning when she got up to go to school. She had been attending school for a full day now for almost two months. Her zest for learning had not been compromised, but her illness had not only changed her view of the world but it had also snatched up the last piece of innocence left lurking in her being. Sophie's school day was about survival. She had to cope with the noise level, as she had severe sound sensitivity, and to do her work when alarms were going off in her head and she didn't know when she would need to go to the nurse to escape the people who seemed to be living inside her head, wreaking havoc.

The following morning Sophie woke up agitated. I could see the anger plastered across her face. She reminded me of a hungry wolf being denied food. She tried to get dressed, but she was holding back something dark from jumping out of her. I watched her as she managed to get dressed and I could see a change coming over her like a dark cloud descending upon the earth right before a tornado hits. She started grunting and growling, emitting sounds without intention or purpose. I knew that she was trying to hold back but it was no use, she sounded like a big black bear fiercely approaching its prey. It was a deep grunting sound that was primeval in nature. There was a darkness in her eyes, an empty barrenness that I could see into, and I knew she was lost.

She began to run around in circles, flailing her arms as these deep, guttural, feral sounds burst forth from her mouth. She was growling at me. It was as if another person had taken over her body and she had been tucked away into safekeeping. Was this rage once again? Where did these animal sounds come from? I needed to contain her so that she did not hurt herself or anyone else. I tried to get eye contact and when I did, I knew that she was in there, deep inside, locked away by the predator that had taken over her body. I told her I loved her, desperate to reach her. She was out of control like nothing I had ever seen before. Sophie's father heard the raucous and came out of the bedroom to take a look. He appeared annoyed by Sophie's behavior and made a comment as if he couldn't fathom the reality that he was facing. He was unable to see beyond his own, unmerciful shadow of self-doubt. He was lost at sea, chasing his denial into the abyss.

I ran to get the Benadryl, hoping that this would help calm her down as it had done so well up until this point in time. It was difficult to administer, as she couldn't stop herself long enough to take the medicine. There was an engine running her around and around in a circle without a direction. Finally, after getting a hold of her and getting the medication into her, I was able to step back and watch as my little girl was consumed by demons. I could see it all slowing down. A caged wild boar had more control than Sophie right at that moment. I successfully got her to go back into her room and lie down as the guttural, wolfish growl slowed down. I held her close as I told her I loved her and that she would be okay. Over and over again, I had held this stranger, begging to have my daughter given back to me. Finally, after this particularly relentless episode, she was able to slowly fall asleep.

I went into the dining room to call the doctor and told Sophie's father he needed to speak to the doctor as well. Together we called Dr. Cameron and explained what had just happened. We told him this had been a rage outburst the likes of which we had never seen. As I recall, he recommended that we take her off the medication and keep her off all medication for a couple of weeks. I agreed with taking her off this medication, but not to staying off all medication. I pleaded with fear in my voice, could she go back on the doxycycline? He suggested we take her off the Prozac and try to contact the psychiatrist as well as to what to do next. I felt as if I had been left on my own, navigating a ship that had no port. Horror gripped me. I hadn't realized that she could get so out of control that she might never return. Dr. Cameron decided to put her back on the doxycycline.

Three hours later Sophie woke up. She reported to me that she was hungry, which I always saw as a good sign. Like a normal sick child at home, she limped around, not feeling up to doing any school work. I let her relax for the rest of the day as I tried to recover from seeing her body and mind being taken over like a zombie in The Walking Dead. Nighttime came and Sophie looked under the weather. She was not her normal self in any way, shape, or form. Peter came home and asked her about her day. Within a few minutes, she exploded

into another episode. The agitated rage hit us from behind and knocked us down like an unexpected ocean
wave. The air was knocked out of us by the shock of it
all. Again, we were back to square one with Sophie. It
was not the questioning that was pushing her to edge of
insanity, but possibly a response to the antibiotic treatment. The Herxheimer (Jarisch-Herxheimer Reaction)
reaction, which has been written about as a reaction of
symptoms worsening under antibiotic treatment, may
have been what was happening. There were just so many
unknowns in Lyme disease that we just couldn't be sure.
The Benadryl was given again and before too long, Sophie was asleep.

The following day we started the doxycycline again.
Since Sophie's reactions were so unpredictable we tried
to get stuff done while she was asleep. We never knew
when the rage would reemerge.

I felt awfully sad. A sadness had seeped into my heart
and had brought me to tears. They were the tears of an
unyielding pain that floated around inside. It traveled
throughout my body, making it hurt in one place and
then another. It was an empty feeling that threatened to
obliterate me into an infinite nothingness.

I looked at Peter sitting next to me, quietly doing his
Sudoku. For him, that was the distraction to beat all
distractions. It allowed him to avoid his pain, my pain,
and the collective pain and sadness that overwhelmed us
when we stopped to let our thoughts enter our conscious
minds, letting us know what was happening. Lyme disease was taking over our daughter's life and our life. We
were in it with her as witnesses, watching an eruption of
bacteria damage a human being. I wanted to scream and
shake it out of her. We had become slaves to this bacte-

rial spirochete. It had come into our life to take us over and destroy us, taking no prisoners. Although its path was treacherous, I believed that it would have an end and that we would get on with it and survive. But life had no promises, no deals in which the outcome was known. We lived every day as if we knew what would happen next. We made promises, deals, and arrangements, believing that we knew what tomorrow would bring. Then we made those promises to our children to make them feel safe and secure in a world that had no safety or security. It was a perpetual lie that we proposed in our daily life to avoid the thorns when we got close enough to smell the roses. Beauty with a sting had captured us unexpectedly.

Peter and I did not speak about what was happening. We just existed next to one another as we tried to survive another day.

Never look back unless you
are planning to go that way.

—Henry David Thoreau

Twelve months passed while we learned to cope with
the unexpected happenings of Lyme disease. The
disease was so much more complicated than most were
willing to acknowledge. The doctors that wanted to help
were fighting the battle for all of the sufferers, trying to
make sound, clinical judgment in an effort to treat people until they were well. Was this not their oath? How
could there be so many barriers preventing doctors from
helping people to get well? It was like being in the middle of the ocean with no compass.

All is experimental when it comes to Lyme disease,
but how it is currently defined limits treatment options.
I was obsessed with finding answers to help my daughter.
Yes, she was going to school and engaging in some activities, but she was still far from the child she had been be-

fore she got sick. She was still miles and miles away from herself. I tried to read everything I could get my hands on to help her. The search consumed me day after day and night after night. I woke up, went to work, came home, and searched the internet. The computer was now my companion. It held the answers that I sought. My life was a rollercoaster that I was unable to get off of. You can travel far and wide and still come up empty-handed when it comes to Lyme disease—at least that was the way I felt about it.

The tears I had shed could fill up the oceans. I held it all inside because I feared that if I burst, there wouldn't be anything left to keep me going, to keep me searching for answers. I had to find the way off this dead-end street. Like a mouse in a maze, I scurried this way and that way, hoping to find my way out.

It was evening and I got into bed next to Peter. He was working on his Sudoku, absorbed in the world of numbers. Engrossed in his activity, he said nothing to me as my body pressed into the mattress next to him. I suspected he believed that Sophie's behavior was not really related to Lyme disease. He just couldn't wrap his head around the idea that bacteria could cross the blood/brain barrier and tear open the part of the brain that controls emotion. There were so many symptoms that emerged from Lyme disease, and each person had varying degrees of the many types of bizarre changes that could occur. I supposed he was unable to fathom how our daughter had become a stranger to us. He wanted to tell her to snap out of it. Her behavior could be so strange. We were a ship lost at sea.

The books and articles I have read about Lyme disease during my daughter's illness and since then have not provided enough information about the disease process or its damage to the body. Yet people continue to suffer, and those who know Lyme disease share the secret camaraderie of prisoners of war.

"She can control it," Peter said suddenly, jerking me out of my reverie about the books that had given me not one ounce of promise for a path to wellness. He went on to rant and rave that she would only get sick when it came to going to school.

How could he be so blind? Did he not know of the sound sensitivity she faced each and every day on the bus—the excruciating sound that pounded away in her head as she sat on the bus as if she were a Lilliputian in the land of the big people in Gulliver's Travels? Why would she act sick for no reason—so sick that she woke up screaming, scared of her own thoughts, immobilized by fear magnified beyond belief? Why would she behave this way without cause? I stared at the ceiling with frustration drumming in my head. This was getting me nowhere. Peter retreated back to his Sudoku; he couldn't argue with a mother who spent all her free time searching for the answer. He lost himself in the numbers again, numbing himself to what his life had become under the strain of our daughter's illness.

Sophie never knew what each day would bring. When she was home sick, she was in bed most of the day resting, always tired. At work I would get phone calls from her telling me that she was scared. I wanted to squeeze the terror right out of her, but on the phone I was helpless, listening to her cry for help. There was no magic wand to bring her back to me. Her little, soft voice begged me to come home and stay with her as she was barely able to tolerate the feeling of fear wrapping itself around her like a boa constrictor. She was walking the tightrope of life and at any moment could fall off into the nightmare that was her reality. I made sure she knew that I would never give up searching for the way to get her well. Her sad eyes tortured my thoughts and stabbed at my heart. The pain of her unfortunate situation dragged me down to an underground world.

Although Sophie seemed to be getting better, I believed we had reached another plateau in the forward movement to wellness, recognizing that making headway with Lyme disease had no clear path. I discussed this with Sophie and Dr. Cameron. Back and forth we went, evaluating Sophie's symptoms, her improvements along the way, and where she was now. It had been almost eighteen months into her antibiotic treatment. We agreed to change the medication to clarithromycin. Again, I was hoping that this would move her toward eradicating the bacteria that had invaded her body in massive proportions. The prescription was filled and we added this to her regimen, which also included Vitamin B for the itching, crawling sensations on her skin, fish oil, a multivitamin, and a probiotic, which she had been taking from the start with the antibiotic treatment.

Not everyone can see the truth, but he can be it.

—Franz Kafka

It was after my sister Amy told me about a raw food expert she had found on YouTube talking about Japanese Knotweed and Lyme disease that my research began to shift. Amy and I talked about the importance of having nutritious food to feed the body and strengthen the immune system. My sister encouraged me to read some books that would shed light on the food issue and recommended The China Study by Colin Campbell.

I was shocked to realize that diet was critical to Sophie's wellness. I had to facilitate a family meeting at home to discuss the food issue and the changes that needed to be made in what we brought into the house and consumed. I knew I had to do everything possible to strengthen Sophie's immune system. Of course there was dissonance amongst the family members, but I knew that nutrition had to be not only considered but also lived when it came to Sophie's overall health and well-ness. If we were going to get her better, we needed to be prepared to try everything, and I would not accept anything less from myself or from my family.

I began to make a daily smoothie. It was a combination of kale, sprouts, apples, bananas, raisins or dates for sweetness, and concentrated green food with other powdered/crushed super fruits thrown into the mix. This became part of the daily routine. I won't say it was easy getting my daughter, who, like most kids, was a chicken nugget and pizza eater, to drink what was essentially green muck on a daily basis. At the beginning she had to close her eyes and pinch her nose to get it down, but after a while it got easier. I told her that this was her medicine too and it had life-saving ingredients, just as much as every other medicine she was taking, and so she drank it. The meals changed too. Slowly we progressed to a different configuration of food on the plate: bigger servings of a greater variety of vegetables and smaller servings of meat. These were challenges that I took seriously to the point that I gave up many foods myself and have never returned to my old eating habits. It didn't matter that others in the house wouldn't do it. I had to do it to prove that it could be done. My love for my child knew no bounds and I would give up whatever I needed to in order to get her better. To be her strength was the only option for me, and I had to let her know with my behavior that we could conquer this illness together.

As I researched online, I came across a YouTube video of a man talking about Japanese Knotweed growing in wooded areas, and explaining that the plant and its root are medicinal sources. This person, Timothy Scott, is a licensed acupuncturist who is trained in Chinese herbal medicine. It was around this time that I also started reading Stephen Harrod Buhner's book Healing Lyme Naturally, which was the first book that gave me a clue as to the microbiology of Lyme disease. The book also identified Timothy Scott as one of the recommended practitioners able to put together the Lyme Protocol of herbs and other ingredients that Buhner's book presents as necessary to heal Lyme disease.

I made an appointment to take Sophie to Brattleboro, Vermont to see Timothy Scott. Together, Sophie and I took this trip of discovery. At Timothy's office, we sat down and told the story of what happened to Sophie up until the present. He did not appear at all surprised by the symptoms I reported to him. He had seen and heard of similar cases like my daughter's. It was a relief to acquire more validation for what was happening to Sophie. Timothy listened to the story, patiently collecting all the details, and responded in a way that eased the distress Sophie and I wore across our faces.

We subsequently made many visits to Timothy's office. During one of our visits, he told us that he, his wife, and his children had all been bitten by ticks and had been on the Lyme Protocol at one time or another, in addition to other herbal supplements. He also authored a book, Invasive Plant Medicine. Timothy made me feel that he was competent in his knowledge of herbal medicine and had a calm, soothing approach during each visit. His perspective was based on seeing many cases of Lyme disease and other tick-borne illnesses, his own personal experience with Lyme disease, and a strong general knowledge base. This generated more hope for Sophie and myself that she could reach a place of wellness.

Timothy talked about the importance of treating the whole person and all of the organ systems. His training lead him to the conclusion that antibiotics primarily focused on killing "bad" bacteria, as he put it, but did not address the significance of strengthening the immune system or the whole person. These conversations had me thinking that attacking this illness by not only targeting the bacteria but also strengthening the body to handle the bacteria on its own was an important key to overall health and wellness.

Moving toward this treatment approach came about when Sophie had reached another plateau in her antibiotic treatment. Although I continued with the antibiotic treatment because I thought it was important to do so, I knew that I also needed to address strengthening her immune system and to continue to confront the problem of the bacteria, as well as detoxification using Timothy's prescribed herbal remedies. I also felt I had to be one step ahead of the illness, and I was always planning what remedy I could try next to help her get well.

Sophie began to take the herbal supplements Timothy recommended. I recall her expressing dissatisfaction that now there was yet another bunch of pills for her to take. Nevertheless, she took the herbs and I, as the gatekeeper, kept her on track with all of these protocols. I believed that the herbal supplements did help to support her immune system and detoxify her body. Throughout the course of the antibiotic treatment and beyond, Sophie continued the herbal protocol. We visited Timothy about every six weeks or so for acupuncture, herbal supports, and ongoing dialogue about her symptoms. Our discussions focused on what symptoms were still present and what symptoms were becoming less prevalent and troublesome. It was difficult to identify what exactly got better and what, if anything, got worse since many of the symptoms reared their ugly head over and over again. As time went on, I recognized that the symptoms occurred with less frequency. If that was a sign of progress, then I was a believer. It was still an enormous feat to look for the good in this situation and see that Sophie really was getting better. Sometimes it had to be pointed out to us that in fact she was improving.

One of the most significant items that stood out in my mind from Timothy Buhner's book was the damage that Lyme disease can do to the immune system. It was frightening to feel that reality hit me like a smack in the face. Absorbing the fact that Lyme disease could always be present had me in a daze for days. It shattered any beliefs I had held dear to me up until this point in time. I knew the damage was done, but not to what extent it would be permanent. I wasn't sure that I would ever be able to figure out Lyme's catastrophe, and I had no belief that there was a doctor out there able to decipher it either. Time was the only healer I could rely upon from this point forward.

Not until we are lost do we begin to understand ourselves.

—Henry David Thoreau

The School Psychologist

Sophie had taken up basketball, and one evening she had a game, but had been unable to attend school during the day. I believed that even though she was ill and could not go to school during the day that she should not be penalized from going to basketball in the evening. School rules do not align with this thinking, so when Sophie walked into the school and the principal saw her, the look we got was one of surprise. She certainly wasn't in favor of my behavior as the parent letting this happen. But I had been devoured by my daughter's illness, so for any pleasure I could suck out of the day, I was willing to do whatever it took to make that happen, even if it meant opposing forces that represented the school authority.

The following day we were called in for a meeting with the principal and the school psychologist. So an appointment was set, and together, Sophie's father and I attended. We got the talk about the rule that if you don't go to school then you don't go to after-school activities. This was interpreted as Sophie manipulating the system. Sophie was still having problems getting through the day at school. The school administrative staff was worried about how to manage Sophie and wanted to know if she was in therapy. There was also discussion raised about Sophie needing to have neuropsychological testing.

Sophie had been attending psychotherapy for about six months during the time she was being seen by the psychiatrist but in the beginning of summer, we stopped therapy. Peter and I agreed that she needed a break. We continued with the psychiatrist and the medication until that was no longer effective. However, when school began after the summer, and the school personnel discovered that Sophie was not in therapy, they were not pleased. Sophie needed a great deal of intervention by school personnel, mainly the principal and the school psychologist, who were directly involved. The school put the pressure on us for Sophie to continue therapy to help with some of her problem behaviors at school— the main problem behavior being that whenever there was a problem I came running to the school and took her home.

But what else could I have done when she was unable to function? Nothing. However, they felt she was becoming too dependent on me and they wanted her to stay in school and work through the difficulties she encountered. Maybe they believed that she wasn't really sick anymore and that her behavior was manipulating me to come and get her when she didn't want to deal with school or what she was feeling. Although I abhorred this idea, I had to consider it a possibility. I agreed that she was dependent, but she was ill too. What were her choices? I had to test the hypothesis so I joined forces with the school staff to help her stay in school to work through the challenges she had to face now that she was getting better. But if I thought that I had to get her, I was going to be at the school to get her and bring her home.

It hurt to hear that when Sophie was upset the school would not let her call me. I hated to hear the pain in her voice as she told me this, even though I understood the reasoning. She had to get through the day at school without me. I knew that I had to let her struggle on her own with the help of the school staff to work it out. I was so wrapped up in her illness that wanting to protect her from it had become my calling. But I knew I had to let her go.

We left the meeting with the principal and the school psychologist with the name of a therapist they recommended. Patricia Wilkins-Vacca, a licensed clinical social worker, was the person we took Sophie to see. Sophie continued to see her and the therapy helped her to explore her feelings about the illness and how she was able to cope with what had happened. She looked forward to her time with Patty. She spent her sessions talking about herself, her family, and how she was going to move beyond the illness. Patty validated Sophie's feelings and helped her to cope with getting better and her fear that she could be attacked by the illness again at any time. Most importantly, she assisted Sophie in recognizing her successes and how far she had come. For this I was grateful.

After our meeting at the school I began the search for a psychologist to do the neuropsychological testing. I was lucky to find a female psychologist from Mt. Sinai Hospital in private practice to conduct the evaluation, which led to Sophie being diagnosed with having sustained a cognitive processing problem. The psychologist believed that this problem would be resolved within a year, but after more than one year, Sophie was still slow at getting her work completed. Her actual academic performance was not damaged, but her processing of information was and still is delayed. This continues to be an issue that we hope will resolve itself at some point in the future. However, we can't be sure that this will ever happen.

The newly acquired information from the neuropsychological evaluation proving that Sophie had a cognitive processing issue led me to search for additional help for my daughter and to discover Neurofeedback.

According to a 2010 New York Times article by Katherine Ellison, Dr. Kerson from the International Society for Neurofeedback and Research, stated, "Neurofeedback is a powerful therapy and should be treated that way." So what is neurofeedback supposed to do? According to the article, "It is a kind of biofeedback for the brain which allows patients to alter their brain waves through practice and repetition." So this is how it works: "You sit in a chair, facing a computer screen while a clinician sticks electrodes to your scalp with a gel-like substance. Wires from the sensors connect to a computer programmed to respond to your brain's activity."

If your brain behaves as desired you get to watch your favorite movie, if not the screen goes blank. At least, that was how neurofeedback was facilitated for Sophie. Training the brain was the key element.

The article suggests that neurofeedback could help with a variety of problems such as anxiety, depression, and Attention Deficit Hyperactivity Disorder. As with many treatments, there is controversy and some confusion over the success of neurofeedback as a treatment. As with all treatments, ongoing research is a necessity. However, in assessing neurofeedback, we need to remember that at one time people thought the world was flat and the person who disagreed and tried to prove otherwise, well, we know what happened to him. The new idea that the world was round was not readily accepted.

Anyway, according to neurofeedback experts, when the brain is properly regulated, it is able to perform better at managing incoming stimuli, which is how I interpreted neurofeedback's benefit for my daughter in addressing the severe anxiety she experienced due to the Lyme bacteria. We found the Hudson Valley Center for Neurofeedback and Sophie attended the recommended sessions. This brought a calming clarity to her brain.

In fact, every treatment helped Sophie along the way. Although it was not easy to separate the variables to determine the exact benefit of each item added to her regimen, each one had its place in her progress. Each individual component added to the complex array of treatments, which helped to stabilize her. I saw changes in her that I was not able to attribute to antibiotic treatment alone, even though antibiotics got her walking again and played a significant role in her getting well. It was a complicated process with answers that were not simple or clearly outlined, but with a multiplicity of treatments, both traditional and alternative, that helped her make progress along the journey to wellness.

During this period, one of the most discomforting symptoms Sophie described was feeling a crawling sensation under her skin. I could only imagine how fear exacerbated this sensation. We could not see it, but Sophie was able to feel it igniting her nerve endings.

"I want to jump out of my skin," she would say.

"I promise you that I will give you something and it will go away," I would reply.

Most often I would give her Benadryl. However, the one item that did end up solving this problem was Vitamin B. Don't ask me how or why, but it took the crawling sensation away permanently. Supplements had an important part to play in aspects of her wellness, and this was one instance where it led to significant results—the elimination of the crawling sensation.

Being lost in the uphill battle of wellness, with its peaks and valleys, frequently had me hanging on a limb of despair. I felt as if I had to bear witness to my daughter's tragedy and the illness that kept torturing her soul. There was not a waking moment or dream state that did not contain some part of this struggle that was trying to break me in half. The cruelty of it all was the lack of understanding and compassion as well as the mystery that surrounded Lyme disease. With the exception of a few professionals, nobody really understood what Sophie was going through.

One day while Peter was standing in the living room looking out the window, he called to me, "Mindy, there's a deer on the lawn." I ran to the front door, opened it to look, and then slammed it shut. The deer stared at me as I watched through the glass window panel, then turned and scurried across the street. Peter continued to stare out the window. "The ticks are out there," he said. I joined him by the window, and as we stood there, look-ing out at the deer innocently picking at scraps of green-ery across the street, he put his arm around me. Finally we were united. At last he was on my side in recognizing the truth of what happened to our daughter. Whether he wanted to admit it or not, he knew that Lyme disease was the perpetrator. Together we stared out the window as I shook my head in agreement. "Yes," I said. "The ticks are out there."

Only the ideas that we really live
have any value.

—Hermann Hesse

The Letter

About one year into Sophie's illness, I was finally able to put together enough courage to question the thought process of the doctors at the pediatric group regarding Lyme disease. I wanted to address the fact that because they had ignored my daughter's tick bites, her life had become an awful mess. So I decided to call the doctor who was the lead person in the group. I left a message for him to call me back and indicated that it was a personal matter related to my daughter's medical care. When the doctor called back, I initially stumbled over my words, not knowing exactly what I wanted to say. The anger was still there inside of me, steaming its way up my throat and ready to spurt out of my mouth. I told myself that I had to retain my composure or the conversation would become a meaningless episode of a mother out of control. How was I going to make a worthwhile conversation happen?

I introduced myself and identified my daughter and the doctor told me that he had the chart in front of him. "Good, I'm glad you have the chart right in front of you," I said. Then I went on to tell him the story of my daughter and the two tick bites. After each tick bite I had taken her to the pediatrician and been told that it was nothing, essentially, and not to worry about it. I asked him, "Do you have the notation there in the record that I discussed the first tick bite?" As I recall, I heard him shuffling paper as he answered, "Yes, I see that it was discussed." I went through the same process when discussing the second tick bite. Again, he agreed that my daughter had been seen and that, in my words, nothing was done.

"Not only was nothing done," I said to him, "but more importantly, it never occurred to any practitioner that I needed to be informed of the signs and symptoms I should be looking out for in case some unusual manifestation of physical ailments began to occur."

To my surprise, the doctor asked, "Well, how is she doing now?"

Okay, I thought, he wasn't going to answer me, was he? "She is doing much better," I said.

"Well, isn't that what matters?" he asked.

"No, that is not good enough," I responded, exasperated. "Yes, I am glad that she is doing better, but not because of anything the doctors in your practice did. Furthermore, not one doctor even warned me of the potential problems and/or symptoms that could manifest from Lyme disease. You didn't even give me a warning. How could you do that?"

I was able to get the words out of me, but somehow I still didn't feel relieved. The doctor said that he was sorry, but that was all he was able to give me. His apology took me back to the beginning of Sophie's Illness, and I could only tell him what a terrible ordeal my daughter had suffered, and expressed my frustration with the fact that the pediatric practice could have helped her but didn't. Did they realize the trauma my daughter suffered? Did anyone care about those suffering the treacherous, jagged edge of Lyme disease and its physically, mentally, and emotionally painful consequences? How was it that we had allowed those in charge to take control and not fight back?

After that conversation, I realized I needed to make all the doctors aware of my daughter's predicament. That was what started me writing a letter to the group. "Dear Doctors," it began. "I want to tell you about a situation regarding my daughter Sophie, who is and has been a patient of yours for quite a number of years." I went on to explain about the tick bites and the response of the pediatric group. Then I told the story of my contact with the lead doctor and his response to me and to my daughter's dilemma. My anger was getting the best of me, but I had to let them know that it was not okay to leave people without a warning. It was the responsibility of the doctors to tell people with children about the problems that could occur because of Lyme disease. It was critical to discuss with their patients, and their patients' parents, the symptoms, both physical and mental, that could manifest. The dissemination of preventative measures was important, but it was not enough. There had to be more information provided about what could happen if the bacteria made your child's body and organ systems its home.

I begged the doctors to do more. I told them it was not enough to stand by and watch the people they intended to help fall off a cliff into the devastating, ravaging illness that is Lyme disease. I wanted them to feel

my anger, my hurt, and my pain. But most of all, I wanted all of those doctors to talk about Lyme disease. Denial
was no longer an option.

Some months later, when I took Sophie for a
physical exam at the pediatric group, we were handed a
never-before-seen brochure about Lyme disease. Could
fighting back have made this happen? At least there was
a warning provided to the helpless mass of parents and
their children who were patients. The brochure was
proof of that.

In the kingdom of the blind, the one-eyed man is king.

—Desiderius Erasmu

Treatment continued as we reached the second year of antibiotics. Again, we were at Dr. Cameron's office for Sophie's regular monthly visit. This was by far one of the better visits we had to endure. We walked into the waiting area as the staff gathered behind the enclosed glass sliding door, eager to see Sophie and find out how she was doing. They seemed to want her to be the ambassador for all the children suffering from Lyme disease. She was their hero on so many levels. They wanted her to tell her story to others.

It was this little, secret push that got me writing Sophie's story. Unfortunately, Sophie was asked to relive the pain over and over again by telling her story. She just wanted to wake up one day and find that Lyme disease had been completely wiped clean from her mind. Sophie wanted to awaken from the nightmare and realize that's all it was, a nightmare. I wanted her to have pure happiness to fill her up. Sophie was glad to feel some joy in her life as she started to get better. It was enough—but only for now. She wanted to get as far away from Lyme disease as she could—and not even outerspace was far enough away for her to escape the horror that ruled her life from one day to the next. She had very few reference points in what was now her eleven years of life to compare the good with the bad. The bad had become all consuming, and I was the one person who was able to hear just how bad it was for her. This was the dilemma: most people's attitudes were, "Don't talk about it and maybe, just maybe, it will all go away." But that day was long overdue.

So every time Sophie entered Dr. Cameron's office, the staff watched her with big smiles on their faces, saying, "Hey, Sophie! How are you today?" She would look up politely and say, "I'm okay." But on that particular day I was unable to help myself. I told them that it had been the best month ever. "Sophie has been doing really well in so many ways and she is so happy," I said. "I never thought I would see her smile again." They all smiled, looking at me with sincere interest and joy for my little girl and me.

That day we met with the physician's assistant. She reviewed what had happened that month. I loved when Sophie wanted to talk, but that day I couldn't help myself and I just blabbered on about how well she was doing—going to school every day for the full day, feeling happier and less anxious. "She still has panic attacks, but she gets over them quicker," I explained. The physician's assistant asked us if we wanted to see Dr. Cameron and I said yes, we would.

Sophie was sitting on the exam table when Dr. Cameron opened the door and smiled at her. "Are you still going to school till twelve p.m. or one p.m.?" he asked. She looked up without a word and watched him in the doorway for a moment, making him wait as always for her response, and then burst out with, "Where have you been all these months? I am in school till two-thirty in the afternoon, which is the end of the day." His smile got even wider.

"Go on and tell Dr. Cameron what you've been doing," I said. Sophie explained that she was also involved in after-school activities as he continued to smile at her and to be happily surprised to hear it all. Dr. Cameron was always jovial and teasing with Sophie, and they had always enjoyed bantering with each other, both verbally and nonverbally. Now that Sophie was doing better, he was sincerely sharing in her joy.

That visit was a long way away from the day when they had first met, with Sophie kicking and screaming in a wheelchair, banging up against the wall of the exam room, telling Dr. Cameron that she did not believe he could help her because no doctor had helped her at the hospital. Dr. Cameron began helping Sophie by allowing her to share with him her deepest, darkest fear of never being able to walk again. He had acknowledged her distress and heard her cry for help. Because of that, they had developed a special language between them that was all their own. Theirs was a glorious, heartfelt partnership.

Dr. Cameron let us know that he had talked with the school nurse and tried to confer the understanding that if Sophie could just get through the episode at school, she would be able to stay for the rest of the time. I explained that we had attended a meeting with the school about that issue and we were trying to work it out together. Things were working, although the first few days had been hard. I knew that I had to let go and allow others to help my daughter.

We continued talking about how Sophie's independence and confidence had been growing. She was slowly returning to the person she had been before the illness. She came home from school each day and did her homework without being pushed or prodded. She wasn't afraid of being by herself, nor was she worrying all the time about being sick, whether she would get fully better or if she would get sick again. Overall, Sophie's fears were lessening even though they weren't totally gone, I reported to Dr. Cameron.

Sophie now had no physical pain anywhere in her body. She had some headaches, but it wasn't clear whether they had anything to do with Lyme disease at this point in time. She had not complained recently of any shooting pains in her legs, arms, or wrists. The shooting pains had been constant yet unpredictable, creeping up on her unexpectedly but often, with a sting that made her scream in pain. It was excruciating for her, and she was overwhelmed by pain that spiraled out of control to the tips of her nerve endings. But now the shooting pains were gone and were hopefully never coming back. Sophie still had headaches, but only once or twice about one to two times a month. And although her anxiety had lessened, it was still not totally eradicated. But life was becoming bearable again for Sophie and for me, and Dr. Cameron was the one medical professional who was helping to guide us out of the messy business of Lyme disease.

Two roads diverged in a wood and I—I took the one less traveled by, and that has made all the difference.

—Robert Frost

The Road To Wellness

Driving in my car with the windows down, pushing through the wind made me feel so powerful. The swooshing noise of the car speeding through the air nearly drowned out the voices on the radio. It didn't matter that I was unable to hear those whispering voices. It was the sound, the power of the wind that I craved. It drowned out any thoughts I had of what had happened to my life.

The trees shading the road, and the woods that stretched for miles beyond, were reminders of the Lyme disease nightmare that haunted me. This beautiful green landscape hid more of those monstrous little ticks that carried the bacteria known as Lyme disease that had changed my daughter's life and mine, forever. I could no longer enjoy the green garden of nature without feeling sadness and trepidation. Only from a distance could I tolerate nature, watching it as I would a movie onscreen at a theater. There was a pain inside of me, a deep, crawling, intruding pain that had sucked the joy from my life, and I didn't know if I would ever recover.

Although Sophie continued to improve, fatigue and anxiety still interfered with her daily life. These symptoms still filled her with despair and sometimes overcame her resilience to forgive and forget all that had happened. The illness was locked up inside her mind as if in a secret box, only to be freed if we could find the magic key. Sophie so desperately wanted to move forward. She wore a façade of tranquility and kept the damage locked away for safekeeping.

I had believed that one day the illness would disappear as quickly as it had arrived. Life makes no promises. I was feeling tired and worn from the relentless struggle of coping with the unpredictability of the illnesses various, reemerging symptoms. I felt as if I was stuck in a hole with no way out. And yet, just as it had from the early onset of symptoms, hope loomed.

As time passed and her symptoms gradually became less severe, less pronounced in ways we could never have imagined, Sophie was able to replicate some normalcy of daily life. However, I continued to wear armor, shielding my little girl from the night terrors that had not subsided. We still had many sleepless nights when she would awaken us with her screaming from earth-shattering nightmares. There was no separating reality from fantasy for her during these episodes. I wondered whether being traumatized by the illness caused the nightmares or if the bacteria were still the originator—manipulating the brain to bring this psychological thriller to life. Whatever the culprit was, Sophie was ready to eradicate this debris from her mind. Psychological duress can lead to a psychiatric disorder known as PTSD. Post-traumatic stress disorder occurs when someone suffers a catastrophic life event that is so emotionally overwhelming that it gets "locked" into the brain, invading the person's life, causing nightmares, flashbacks, and panic. Depending upon the severity of the trauma, those feelings, which are ultimately unmanageable, can result in explosive anger, paranoia, and intense, fearful helplessness.

I knew I had to be the protector, keeping the monsters away that trapped her while she was deep in sleep. Would the nightmares ever go away permanently? Were they a prelude to a future of further torture? I hoped the nightmares would have an end. When that occurred, I knew that I needed to retreat, to allow my daughter to manage the nighttime by herself. I would have to readjust my role, but not without scars marking my memory.

Sophie was facing the betrayal of the human condition and what that brings. She had been exposed to and had witnessed how Lyme took her life and shaped it into something else. Sophie had fought long and hard, with her will to survive unscathed. I felt unable to imagine others suffering the way she did, constantly feeling defeated and yet still managing to hope for a remedy.

Two years and six months had passed. "Mom, do you remember when I was in the hospital and one of the doctors said that maybe I was having a growth spurt?" she asked. "Yes, I do remember that," I said. "Wasn't that a ridiculous remark?" Sophie asked. "How could they say a growth spurt?" She was exasperated by the absurdity of it all, by the guessing game that had been played with her life.

We stared at each other for a long moment. Then she turned her head to the side and asked, "Mom, what are you looking at?" I replied, "I am looking at you, silly." I went on to say, "I can't believe we are here, like this, talking about the hospital. It is a miracle that you have come so far forward from this awful disease and I am so grateful."

Sophie smiled at me as I spoke, and I felt my heart soar. I would give anything to keep that smile on her face and never have to look back at what we've been through. We may never be sure of a cure, but I know that I did my utmost to help my little girl—and that "I took the [road] less traveled by/and that has made all the difference."

I have always believed, and
still believe, that whatever
good or bad fortune may
come our way, we can always
give it meaning and transform
it into something of value.

—Hermann Hesse

Sophie was on antibiotics for almost three years, and
stopped taking them almost to the exact day she had
started. Then it was time to see whether her immune
system could take over and do the work on its own. Six
months after stopping the antibiotics, there were no

symptoms plaguing her body. She was still working on building her strength and stamina but she was no longer collapsing into a bedridden fatigue or anything near that. There was no physical pain in any part of her body, no anxiety left to torture her mind. Happiness emanated from her. She often wore a grin that stretched from one cheek to the other. Worry had taken a long vacation from her life—and from our family's lives. Our daughter, Sophie, as we had always known her, had returned to us. Her letter, below, proves that.

"I am Sophie and I am now thirteen years old. My life is far from perfect. I worry most of the time. Well, not all the time. I worry about doing well in school, how other kids will treat me, and getting sick again from Lyme disease. I worry about something bad happening to my parents. My mom is my hero. She saved my life. My family is the most important thing to me. I hope that when I grow up I will be able to do something to help people get better from Lyme disease and other illnesses.

People always ask me about what happened. Well, it's hard to talk about it. I feel embarrassed about the way I behaved. My therapist tells me that the person then was not me, but what Lyme disease made me. People want to know whether I read the story my mom wrote about me. Truth be told, no, I did not read it, I lived it and I don't want to go back there, ever."

—Sophie

RESOURCES

Books on Lyme Disease

Cure Unknown, by Pamela Weintraub (St. Martin's Griffin, 2009)

Healing Lyme, by Stephen Buhner (Raven Press, 2005)

Lab 257, by Michael Christopher Carroll (Harper Collins Publisher, 2004)

Out of the Woods, by Katina I. Makris, CCH, CIH (Elite Books, 2011)

Books and Websites on Health and Wellness

The China Study, by T. Colin Campbell, Ph.D. & Thomas M. Campbell II, M.D. (BenBella Books, 2004)

Prevent and Reverse Heart Disease, Caldwell B. Esselstyn Jr., M.D. (Penguin Group, 2007)

The UltraMind Solution, by Mark Hyman, M.D.

Hippocrates Health Institute: hippocratesinst.org

Dr. Mercola: mercola.com

www.thelivingseed.com

Book and Website on Herbals

Invasive Plant Medicine, by Timothy Scott (Healing Arts Press, 2010)

Green Dragon Botanicals: greendragonbotanicals.com

Alternative Treatments

The Hudson Valley Center for Neurofeedback: hvcnf.com

Lyme Disease Professional Organizations

International Lyme and Associated Diseases Society: ilads.org
Lyme Disease Network: lymenet.com
lymedisease.org (formerly CALDA)
Lyme Disease Association, Inc.: lymediseaseassociation.org
Lyme Project: lymeproject.com

Healthcare Practitioners

Patricia Wilkins Vacca LCSW: patriciawilkins-vacca.com
Mark Goldhirsch, D.C.: drmarkg.com
Dr. Mark Hyman: drhyman.com
Dr. Daniel J Cameron: www.lymeproject.com
Timothy Scott: www.greendragonbotanicals.com

Articles on the Web

Jaslow, Ryan. "Curbing CT Scans in Kids Could Cut Cancer Risk," *cbsnews.com*. June 10, 2013. Web.
URL: www.cbsnews.com/news/curbing-ct-scans-in-kids-could-cut-cancer-risk

Ellison, Katherine; "Neurofeedback Gains Popularity and Lab Attention," *nytimes.com*. October 4, 2010, Web.
URL: www.nytimes.com/2010/10/05neurofeedback.html

CPSIA information can be obtained at www.ICGtesting.com
Printed in the USA
BVOW05s1640190516

448559BV00002B/36/P